T5-BQA-839

A BIBLIOGRAPHICAL ESSAY

ON THE

HISTORY OF THE SOCIETY OF JESUS

This book is Number 6 in

Series IV: Study Aids on Jesuit Topics

WILLIAM V. BANGERT, S.J.

A BIBLIOGRAPHICAL ESSAY

ON THE

HISTORY OF THE SOCIETY OF JESUS

Books in English

THE INSTITUTE OF JESUIT SOURCES

St. Louis, 1976

IMPRIMI POTEST: Very Reverend Leo F. Weber, S.J.
Provincial of the Missouri Province
April 29, 1976

IMPRIMATUR: Most Reverend Charles R. Koester
Vicar General of St. Louis
May 13, 1976

271.5
B224

79030813

© 1976   The Institute of Jesuit Sources
Fusz Memorial, St. Louis University
3700 West Pine Blvd.
St. Louis, Missouri 63108

All rights reserved
Printed in the United States of America
Library of Congress Catalog Card Number: 76-12667
ISBN 0-912422-16-5

To the Jesuit novices from New York to California
and from Minnesota to Louisiana,
good companions on the highway of Jesuit history

Published through the aid of funds
donated by the late Mr. James L. Monaghan
of Milwaukee, Wisconsin,
1867 - 1963,
in memory of his brother,
Reverend Edward V. Monaghan, S.J.,
1879 - 1922.

C O N T E N T S

ON SERIES IV: STUDY AIDS ON JESUIT TOPICS

For some twenty-five years the author of the present
work, Father William V. Bangert, S.J., has been teaching
the history of the Society of Jesus and European history
to Jesuit scholastics, first at St. Andrew-on-Hudson and
recently as visiting lecturer in most of the Jesuit novi-
tiates of the United States. He is also well known as the
author of the scholarly and comprehensive *A History of the
Society of Jesus*, the respected biography *To the Other
Towns: A Life of Blessed Peter Favre*, and articles in
periodicals and encyclopedias. Because of the wide reading into which this work has carried him, his friends and
students have asked him over and over again for lists of
books, with his opinion about them, either on Jesuit history as a whole or some segment of it. This led him to
attempt to draw up such a list which he could send out
whenever such requests came. The Institute of Jesuit
Sources is now pleased to make this list available to a
public wider still by publishing it as Number 6 in its
Series IV: Study Aids on Jesuit Topics.

It seems advisable to state the rationale of Series
IV in each volume published in it. The series is an effort to solve various aspects of the following problem.

From its inception the Institute of Jesuit Sources
has been oriented toward the publishing of scholarly books
of quality. Such books, carefully selected, obviously
have advantages, especially the long-lasting values aris-
ing from their presence in libraries. But this orientation,

if maintained exclusively, also entails two disadvantages which are especially hampering and costly in our present era of rapid developments and changes: the lengthy time required for the writing and editing, and the expense of typesetting, printing, and binding with cloth.

There is another class of writings, such as doctoral dissertations, study aids, bibliographies, monographs, preliminary editions, and documented or well founded reflections, which have a different but genuine value. These are, in many cases, not yet the finished, polished, and fully matured scholarship ordinarily found in the volumes published by university presses. But they are a step toward such scholarship. They contain much sound material which is truly helpful to interested persons and which would remain unavailable if postponed until high perfection could be attained. In many cases such delay could all too easily turn out to be an instance in which the dreamed of best, which may never come, is the enemy which defeats the presently attainable good.

This new Series IV will consist of studies in this category. Hopefully, too, it will offer some solution of the problem sketched above. An effort will be made to keep the books or booklets inexpensive through the use of typewriter composition and paperback bindings. Editorial time and cost, too, will be kept as low as possible, with the responsibility for details being allowed to rest more fully on the authors than on the editors of the Institute of Jesuit Sources.

In the designing of this new series, many helpful ideas have been taken from the somewhat similar procedure in scholarly publishing which has been launched by the Council on the Study of Religion, for example, in the two "Dissertation Series" respectively of the American Academy of Religion and of the Society of Biblical Literature. The rationale of these series is well described by Robert

W. Funk and Robert A. Spivey in the *Bulletin for the Council on the Study of Religion*, Volume IV, number 3 (June, 1973), pages 3-13, 28-29, and 36-37; and also, at greater length, in the *Report of the Task Force on Scholarly Communication and Publication*, edited by George W. MacRae, S.J. (1972, available from the Council on the Study of Religion Executive Office, Waterloo Lutheran University, Waterloo, Ontario, Canada). Indebtedness to this helpful information and example is gratefully acknowledged.

George E. Ganss, S.J.
Director and General Editor
The Institute of Jesuit Sources

A U T H O R ' S   P R E F A C E

The purpose of this bibliographical essay is modest.
It is to provide a short critique of books in English on
the history of the Society of Jesus. Books in foreign
languages are therefore not included, except where they
have been translated into English. Older works, such as
the lives of Jesuit saints by Francis Goldie, are omitted
save where no newer works have appeared to supplant them.
Periodical literature is also omitted, except in a few
rare instances where few or no books have appeared on a
particular area of Jesuit history.

These restrictions mean the exclusion of some of the
best literature on Jesuit history, but the incorporation
of articles and literature in foreign languages would push
this essay to the proportions of a multi-volume work. Besides, this essay is meant to be of service to those who
would be more attracted to reading a work in English rather
than in, say, German, Portuguese, Italian, or Spanish.

Another restriction dictated by space is the exclusion,
except for some general works on the history of Jesuit spirituality, of the writings of Jesuits on asceticism and
mysticism. This means the omission of such significant
figures as Luis de la Puente, Jean Surin, Louis Lallemant,
Jeremias Drexel, and a host of others whose spiritual literature has been translated into English. This category
within the Society's history calls for a bibliographical
essay of its own.

Among the volumes included in this essay are some
whose purpose is more broad than Jesuit history but which
give a significant number of pages to the Society. I have
in mind such works as C. R. Boxer's *Christian Century in
Japan*, in which the Society has a central role. Some of the

xiii

best writing about Jesuit history is in volumes of this kind.

Under the heading *Biographies* I include autobiographies, editions of correspondence, spiritual journals, and diaries. Those volumes that subsequently appeared in a paperback edition have an asterisk at the end of the title. Paperback originals have a double asterisk.

A bibliographical essay carries within itself an inherent weakness. It presents the critique of the author only, a critique that can differ sharply with the judgment of others. The ideal would be to present a survey of the varying judgments on each title, but limitations of space make this impractical. But one person's judgment can do at least what a plain, non-committal bibliography cannot do. It gives the potential reader, especially the uninitiated, some idea of the terrain he is entering.

Three Jesuits have given me professional assistance in this work. They are Fathers Charles Polzer of Arizona, W. F. Rea of Rhodesia, and Michael Shields of Canada. I wish to thank them publicly.

I hope that this tool will give extensive service to those who wish to deepen their understanding of Jesuit history.

William V. Bangert, S.J.

A BIBLIOGRAPHICAL ESSAY

ON THE

HISTORY OF THE SOCIETY OF JESUS

PART I. BIBLIOGRAPHIES

The best work in this area is *Bibliography of the
History of the Society of Jesus*, edited by László Polgár,
S.J. (Rome and St. Louis, 1967). *Bibliography of the English Province of the Society of Jesus*, edited by Edmund F.
Sutcliffe, S.J. (London, 1957) is a valuable guide on literature about the English Jesuits. *Contemporary Trends in
Studies on the Constitutions of the Society of Jesus. An-
notated Bibliographical Orientations* ** by Ignacio Iparra-
guirre, S.J., translated by Daniel F. X. Meenan, S.J. (St.
Louis, 1974) is a valuable collection of 134 titles of the
more important works and articles on the Jesuit *Constitutions*, with a brief résumé of the core of each book listed.

---

*   A single asterisk indicates a subsequent paperback
    edition.
** A double asterisk indicates a paperback original.

A *History of the Society of Jesus* by William V. Bangert,
S.J. (St. Louis, 1972) is the most comprehensive one-volume
account of the Society's history, incorporating much of the
recent historical research on the Society. It concludes
with a brief account of General Congregation XXXI (1965-
1966) and an Epilogue. *An Introduction to Jesuit Life.
The Constitutions and History through 435 Years* * by Thomas
H. Clancy, S.J., (St. Louis, 1976) is a rapid survey of the
Jesuit Constitutions and key events and turning points in
Jesuit history, presented in a quick-moving narrative. It
includes accounts of General Congregations XXXI (1965-1966)
and XXXII (1974-1975) as well as five appendices on specialized subjects in Jesuit life. *The Jesuits 1534-1921*
by Thomas J. Campbell, S.J. (2 volumes, New York, 1921; re-
issued Boston, 1971) is outdated and poorly organized in
parts. *The Jesuits* by Martin P. Harney, S.J. (New York,
1941) is a generally reliable compendium but some chapters
are overpacked with names of men whose relative significance
is not made clear. As a consequence the narrative is often
dense and difficult to read. Denis Meadows' *Obedient Men*
(New York, 1954) is sketchy and superficial. Rambling and
disjointed, *St. Ignatius and the Jesuits* by Theodore Maynard (New York, 1956) lacks genuine penetration and understanding. The *Power and Secret of the Jesuits* by René
Fülöp-Miller, translated by F. S. Flint and D. F. Tait
(New York, 1930), while readable, is journalistic and
anecdotal in character. In its penchant for the sensation-
al and in its failure as a serious and reliable historical
account, it does not reveal "the power and secret" of the
Jesuits. Heinrich Boehmer's *The Jesuits*, translated by
Paul Z. Strodach (Philadelphia, 1928) is in the author's
own words "a brief historical monograph." It moves hardly
beyond the early 17th century. Overfacile generalizations,

2

with accompanying failures in accuracy, are prevalent.
The Jesuits by Christopher Hollis (New York, 1968) has
many inaccuracies and misspellings, is rambling and poorly
organized, and presents judgments that lack balanced historical nuances. *The Founding of the Jesuits* by Michael
Foss (London, 1969), despite some valuable and illuminating insights, is flawed by uneven narrative, imprecise
political background, undocumented quotations, and extrav-
agant generalizations. The title is misleading, since the
author does not concentrate on the origins of the Society
but rather discusses various issues in the full sweep of
Jesuit history. Starting with volume 12 and continuing
to volume 40 Ludwig von Pastor in his *History of the Popes
from the Close of the Middle Ages*, translated by Ralph
Francis Kerr, Ernest Graf, O.S.B., E. F. Peeler, (St. Louis,
1902-1953) gives considerable attention to the Society in
its development and activity within the broad context of
ecclesiastical history. The Society receives extended attention in five volumes of Henri Daniel-Rops' *History of
the Church of Christ: The Catholic Reformation*, translated
by John Warrington (Garden City, 1964); *The Church in the
Seventeenth Century*, translated by J. J. Buckingham (New
York, 1963); *The Church in the Eighteenth Century*, translated by John Warrington, (New York, 1964); *The Church in
an Age of Revolution 1789-1870*, translated by John Warrington (New York, 1965); *A Fight for God 1870-1939*, translated
by John Warrington (New York, 1966). These volumes, while
readable, tend to be uncritical and defensive, and to give
France an overproportionate amount of attention. James
Brodrick, S.J., in his *The Origin of the Jesuits* * (New
York, 1940) has produced a work close to the sources and
graceful in its literary style, closing with the death of
St. Ignatius. The *Progress of the Jesuits* (New York, 1947)
by the same author is not so much a history of the Society
during the period 1556-1580 as a colorful narrative about

3

selected aspects of that history. *Fasti Breviores* by P. J.
Chandlery, S.J. (London, 1910) is what the complete title
describes it to be: a daily record of memorable events in
the history of the Society of Jesus. It is frequently
marred by mistakes. H. Outram Evennett, a distinguished
scholar of Cambridge University, presents two short, del-
icately nuanced, and gracefully written pictures of the
Jesuits within a broad historical context. The first, in
Chapter IX, "The New Religious Orders," of *The New Cambridge
Modern History*, Volume II (Cambridge, 1968), goes to the
death of St. Ignatius. The second, in Chapter V, "The
Counter-Reformation," of *The Reformation Crisis* *, edited
by Joel Hurstfield (London, 1965), takes the study into
early 17th century. *The Spirit of the Counter-Reformation*
by H. Outram Evennett, edited by John Bossy (Cambridge,
1968) consists of the Birkbeck Lectures that Evennett gave
at the University of Cambridge in May, 1951. This work is
a study of major importance, in which the author gives
prominent place to the role of the Jesuits in the formation of the spiritual attitudes of the Catholic Church
during the 16th and 17th centuries. A Postscript is con-
tributed by John Bossy, the editor, some of whose historical judgments on the Society are farfetched and simplistic.
David Knowles writes the Foreword in a sensitive tribute
to the person and work of Evennett. *The Counter Reformation 1559-1610* by Marvin O'Connell (New York, 1974) is
Volume IV of the *Rise of Modern Europe* series and contains
about 15 scattered pages on the Society as well as other
references to individual Jesuits. There are some factual
errors, such as identifying Claudio Aquaviva as a Spaniard.
As is the general character of the volumes in the *Rise of
Modern Europe* series, the presentation is in the form of
a historical essay that presupposes a knowledge of the
main facts rather than a straight narrative account. Each
of the volumes in this series contains a bibliographical

essay. Some of the titles in Father O'Connell's essay are
either unreliable or do not represent the best of modern
research. *The Jesuits. Their Spiritual Doctrine and Prac-*
tice * by Joseph de Guibert, S.J., translated by William
J. Young, S.J. and edited by George E. Ganss, S.J. (Chicago, 1964 and St. Louis, 1972) is a historical study of the
spirituality of the Society. Although it is not a completely refined and finished work, since the author died
suddenly in 1942, it is an impressive achievement and is
essential for an understanding of the historical implementation of St. Ignatius' spiritual heritage. Father de
Guibert's mastery of the 16th and 17th centuries is more
sure than that of the 18th, 19th and 20th centuries. *Post-*
Reformation Spirituality by Louis Cognet, translated by P.
Hepburne Scott (New York, 1959), a short work, has about
fifteen pages devoted exclusively to the Society besides
many passages about individual Jesuits. This work, by an
eminent French Oratorian scholar, has a special value in
as much as it places Jesuit spirituality within the historical context that also includes the Carmelites, Cardinal de Bérulle, Philip Neri, Benet Caulfield, and others.
There is no index. *Christian Spirituality* by Pierre Pourrat,
4 volumes, translated by W. H. Mitchell (New York, 1927),
a basic tool for the study of spiritual doctrine through
the ages, devotes much space in Volumes 3 and 4 to the
history of the Society's spirituality. *A Literary History*
of Religious Thought in France from the Wars of Religion
down to our Own Times by Henri Bremond, 2 volumes, translated by K. L. Montgomery (New York, 1928 and 1930) are
the only two translated volumes of this 12-volume classic.
The Jesuits appear prominently in Volume 1, which stresses
their part in the creation and spread of the Devout Humanism
of early 17th century France. *From Pachomius to Ignatius.*
A Study in the Constitutional History of the Religious
Orders by David Knowles (Oxford, 1966), the Sarum Lectures

5

at Oxford during 1964-1965, places the Society's foundation
within the context of the constitutional tradition of religious life within the Church. Knowles, a skilled historian, does this especially in the chapter entitled "Tran-
sition to the Modern World." The style, while clear, is
very compact and concentrated. *Studies in the Spirituality
of Jesuits* (St. Louis, 1969-   )has some issues that treat
historical questions. These are "The Authentic Spiritual
Exercises of St. Ignatius: Some Facts of History and Ter-
minology Basic to their Functional Efficacy Today" (Vol. I,
no. 2, November, 1969) by George E. Ganss, S.J.; "The General Congregations of the Society of Jesus: A Brief Survey
of their History" (Vol. VI, no. 1 and 2, January and March,
1974) by John W. Padberg, S.J.; "The Deliberation that
Started the Jesuits. A Commentary on the *Deliberatio pri-
morum Patrum*. Newly Translated, with a Historical Introduction" (Vol. VI, no. 4, June, 1974) by Jules J. Toner, S.J

A. *The Missions*

Jesuits are strongly present in *A History of the Expansion of Christianity*. Volume III *Three Centuries of
Advance, A.D. 1500-A.D. 1800* by Kenneth Scott Latourette
(New York, 1939). This volume covers the missionary effort in Asia, Africa, and the Americas. The author, a non-
liturgical, evangelical Protestant makes a genuine effort
to appreciate the Jesuit endeavor. The strength of the
work is in its comprehensive picture; its weakness is in
its thinness and lack of depth. *A History of Christian
Missions* by Stephen Neill (Baltimore, 1964) gives a straight
forward and critical consideration of the Society's role
on the missions. The author of this volume, No. 6 in *The
Pelican History of the Church*, was an Anglican bishop in
India. *Beyond All Horizons*, edited by Thomas J. M. Burke,

S. J. (Garden City, 1957) is a collection of 12 essays by Jesuits and others on the theme of Jesuits in the foreign mission fields of both earlier centuries and the present. Some of the essays are disappointingly thin, and, despite a common theme, fail to interlock into a cohesive unity.

The Jesuits by Archbishop Alban Goodier, S.J. (New York, 1930), a short work of eighty-four pages, is an essay on the interior spirit of St. Ignatius and the Society and their attitudes toward prayer and work rather than a narrative history. *The Jesuits In Modern Times* by John La Farge, S.J., (New York, 1928) is addressed to those of the 1920's "who, though versed in current issues and alive to current ethical and social discussions, have yet to find an informed presentation of the Jesuit's aim in life in the terms characteristic of such discussions in our time and country." *Jesuit Spirit in Time of Change*, edited by Raymond A. Schroth, S.J. (Westminster, Md., 1968) is a collection of thirteen essays by modern Jesuits, some scholarly, some popular, and with varying relevance to the Society. Some of the titles are: "The Ignatian Experience as Reflected in the Spiritual Theology of Karl Rahner," "St. Ignatius' Intuitions on Obedience and Their Written Juridical Expression," "The Liturgical Word--The Spiritual Exercises--The Jesuit Response," "Harlem Diary." *The New Jesuits*, edited by George Riemer (Boston, 1971) is a series of interviews, uneven in depth and value, with eleven American Jesuits of the 1960's. *The Jesuit in Focus* by James Daly, S.J. (Milwaukee, 1940) is a collection of twenty-six informal essays, casual and personal in style, about such topics as "The Jesuit Lay Brother," "Persecutions," "The Old Society and the New," "The Embittered Ex-Jesuit." The tone is often apologetic and defensive. *The Jesuits. A Self-Portrait* by Peter Lippert, S.J., translated by John Murray (New York, 1958) is a series of reflections in thirteen short chapters by an experienced spiritual director on the interior spirit that holds the members of the Society together in one body. The chapters treat such topics as "Letter and Spirit," "Personality and Service," "The Mysticism of Action."

A.   The Enlightenment

Research in Jesuit history of the 17th and 18th centuries is in no way comparable with that which has been done on the origins of the Society in the 16th century. Relatively little has been done. The picture of the Society during the Enlightenment and Suppression therefore remains imprecise. *Catholics and Unbelievers in Eighteenth Century France* * by Robert R. Palmer (Princeton, 1939) is the best, although inadequate, account of Jesuit involvement in the philosophical and theological issues of the 18th century. Palmer contends that of all the Catholics in France of the 18th century the Jesuits were the best equipped intellectually and the most disposed to try to bridge the chasm between the Church and the *philosophes*. Jesuits appear frequently in *The Bourgeois. Catholicism vs Capitalism in Eighteenth-Century France* by Bernard Groethuysen, translated by Mary Ilford (New York, 1968). This work surveys the ways ideas on God, death, hell, salvation, work, money were presented by the spiritual leaders of the day. It is seriously flawed by the lack of an index and inadequate identification of several of the persons who appear in the narrative. Two excellent studies of two prominent French Jesuits and their part in the world of the Enlightenment appear in *Studies on Voltaire and the Eighteenth Century*, edited by Theodore Besterman (Geneva, 1957 and 1969). The first is "Berthier's Journal de Trévoux and the Philosophers" by John N. Pappas. It is about the Jesuit editor of the Society's *Journal de Trévoux*, Father Guillaume Berthier, and appears in volume III of the *Studies* (1957). The second is "A Study of the Works of Claude Buffier" by Kathleen S. Wilkins, which appears in volume LXVI of the *Studies* (1969). The title *Jesuits and Jacobins. Enlightenment and Enlightened Despotism in*

Austria by Paul P. Bernard (Urbana and Chicago, 1971) is misleading, since the work has a wider scope than suggested. While it presents considerable information about Austrian Jesuits and their contacts with the Enlightenment, especially after the suppression of the Society, it nevertheless has a scattered effect and lacks the pointedness of a comprehensive synthesis.

B. *The Suppression and Restoration*

The single best account of the suppression and restoration is in volumes 36 to 40 of Ludwig von Pastor's *The History of the Popes*, translated by E. F. Peeler (St. Louis, 1949-1953). These volumes are translations of volume 16 of the German, which was done by W. Wühr, J. Schmidlin, Vierneisel, Wilhelm Kratz, S.J., and Karl Kneller, S.J., from the notes of von Pastor. Readable but prosaic in style, these volumes are rich in detail. Another account, shorter, older but reliable, is a series of 19 articles in *The Month* (volumes 99-102, 1902-1903) entitled "The Suppression of the Society of Jesus" by Sydney Smith, S.J. *The Suppression of the Society of Jesus in the Portuguese Dominions* by Alfred Weld, S.J. (London, 1876) is a clear and straightforward account with several fine quotations from contemporary correspondence and records but it is flawed by a polemical style. *The Expulsion of the Jesuits from Latin America* **, edited by Magnus Mörner (New York, 1965), is a collection of short essays, some critical, some laudatory, of the Society's role in South American history. Among the contributors is the eminent octogenarian, Guillermo Furlong, S.J., who writes of the Jesuits as "the heralds of democracy" through their teaching of Suarezian political thought. *Philippine Jesuits in Exile. The Journals of Francisco Puig, S.J., 1768-1770* by Nicholas

B. *The Suppression and Restoration*

Cushner, S.J. (Rome, 1964), a work of careful scholarship, gives a vivid insight into the hardships suffered by the Spanish Jesuits during their expulsion from the Philippines. The best brief, comprehensive, and up-to-date survey of the suppression is "The Second Centenary of the Suppression of the Jesuits" in *Thought* (Volume 48, 1973, 165-188) by William V. Bangert, S.J.

PART V.   SPECIAL AREAS

A.   Africa

Works in English about the Society in Africa are scarce
Most deal with the 19th and 20th centuries. This is under-
standable, since the Society before 1773 took vital root in
but few areas of Africa. An important work among those recently published is *Gubulawayo and Beyond. Letters and Journals of the Early Jesuit Missionaries in Zambesia, 1879-1887*
edited by Michael Gelfand (London, 1968). The editor, for
the most part, lets the missionaries speak for themselves.
This volume records not only a tale of heroism but also the
failure to comprehend the principles of missionary adaptation by men who were seemingly unaware of the Ricci and De
Nobili tradition in the Society. Most of the material in
Diaries of the Jesuit Missionaries at Bulawayo 1879-91 **,
translated from the French (Salisbury, Rhodesia, 1958), is
found in Gelfand's volume. Father W. F. Rea, S.J., with
his extensive and scholarly knowledge of the Catholic
Church in Africa, is the author of several small, reliable
works that include *Seventy-Five Years in Two Cities. The
Story of St. George's* ** (Salisbury, Rhodesia, 1971), which
records the history of the Jesuit College in Salisbury;
*George Westbeech and the Barotseland Missionaries 1878-
1888* ** (Salisbury, Rhodesia, 1968), the account of the
foundation and failure of the first Catholic mission to
Zambia; *70 Years 1892-1962. The Story of the Chishawasha
Mission* ** (Salisbury, Rhodesia, 1962). Father Rea's doctoral thesis, *The Economics of the Zambezi Mission 1580-
1759*, about to go to print in Lisbon, is the first account
in English of the Society's pre-suppression missions in
south Africa. Four-fifths of this work treat the Jesuit
missions, one fifth the Dominican. *Portuguese Voyages
1498-1663*, edited by Charles D. Ley (London, 1947), contains the vivid description by the Portuguese Jesuit

Jerónimo Lobo of the origin of the Blue Nile, which he saw
in 1628, some 150 years before the Englishman James Bruce
claimed to be the first European to have visited this spot.
The translation has an interesting history of its own.
Abbé Joachim Le Grand translated Lobo into French. Dr.
Samuel Johnson made an abridged translation of Le Grand's
work. It was Johnson's first published book. *African
Angelus. Episodes and Impressions* by C. C. Martindale, S.J.
(London, 1932), although not a history, contains considerable information about past and present missions of the
Society in Africa. This volume is a chatty, informal account of the author's travels in Africa in 1931. It is
flawed by the absence of an index. *Irish Jesuits in Northern Rhodesia* and *Irish Jesuits among the Mild Batonga* by
J. Sweeney, S.J. (both Dublin, 1954) are schematic accounts,
each only 24 pages in length, of modern Jesuit missionary
enterprises.

B. South America

   Latin America. An Historical Survey by Peter Masten
Dunne, S.J., and John F. Bannon, S.J. (Milwaukee, 1947),
a work intended for the classroom (944 pages) and without
pretense at creative scholarship, gives solid information
about the Jesuit endeavor, placing it within the broad
historical context of the Americas. In his well-written,
clear, and scholarly *Spanish Policy in Colonial Chile. The
Struggle for Social Justice, 1535-1700* (Stanford, 1968),
Eugene H. Korth, S.J., gives a prominent part to the Jesuits,
especially Father Diego de Torres Bollo and Father Luis de
Valdivia. *The Lost Paradise* by Philip Caraman, S.J., (London, 1975) is the best and most up-to-date general survey
of the Jesuits' work in the Reductions of Paraguay. In a
consistently readable and frequently vivid narrative,

Father Caraman presents the fruit of many years of research
and travel. *Golden Years on the Paraguay* by George O'Neill,
S.J., (London, 1934) remains a valuable straightforward account of the Reductions. An older work on the Reductions,
most sympathetic but without the advantage of modern research, is *A Vanished Arcadia* by Robert Gallinigad Bontine
Cunninghame Graham (London, 1901; New York, 1924), an explorer and writer with an intimate knowledge of that part
of South America. Highly specialized in its concentration
on different problems faced by the Jesuits is Magnus Mörner'
*The Political and Economic Activities of the Jesuits in the
La Plata Region: The Hapsburg Era,* translated by Albert
Read (Stockholm, 1953), in which Mörner usually allows the
documents to speak for themselves. Since this volume was
originally written for Swedes, it includes much introductory
material on the Society of Jesus and the Spanish colonial
empire. *The Masters and the Slaves. A Study on the Development of Brazilean Civilization* by Gilberto Freyre, translated by Samuel Putnam (New York, 1946) is a widely ac-
claimed work, sociological in bent, that considers three
elements in Brazil's first centuries of growth: the Portuguese conqueror, the aboriginal Indian, the imported Negro.
Freyre judges that Jesuit methods of Christianization "were
not always the most intelligent, the most Christian, or
most humane ones." Jesuit scholars react differently.
Father Serafim Leite feels that Freyre is anti-Catholic;
Father Alves Correia agrees with some of Freyre's criti-
cisms. In the second edition of this work (New York, 1956),
Freyre defends himself, claiming that he aims simply to
halt the uncritical adoration of the Jesuits. In *The Golden
Age of Brazil 1695-1750* (Berkeley, 1962) Charles R. Boxer
with his characteristic order and lucidity links the Jesuits
to many of the key problems of the Portuguese South American colony. He shows, for example, that many Jesuit missionaries, including the great Antonio Vieira, made a

distinction between the enslavement of American Indians
and African blacks, condemning the former practice and con-
doning the latter. *King and Church: The Rise and Fall of
the Patronato Real* by W. Eugene Shiels, S.J. (Chicago, 1961)
has as its primary purpose to make available in original
and in translation the documents that relate how the King
of Spain came to be empowered to be the vicar of the Vicar
of Christ in the Americas. Since the Jesuits of the pre-
suppression in the Americas had to work within the structure of the Royal Patronage, the volume throws light on the
difficulties the Society had to face, especially the royal
absolutism of the 18th century. This work makes difficult
reading. *The Intellectual Conquest of Peru. The Jesuit
College of San Pablo, 1568-1767* by Luis Martin (New York,
1968) is an excellent portrayal, scholarly and clearly
written, of the history of the oldest Jesuit school in
South America, San Pablo of Lima, and its vital role in
the cultural life of Peru.

C.   Central and North America: Spanish Influence

Jesuits appear prominently in *Cycles of Conquest: The
Impact of Spain, Mexico, and the United States on the Indians of the Southwest, 1533-1960* by Edward Spicer (Tucson,
(1963). This work, written in non-technical language, rep-
resents a notable effort at historical synthesis by an an-
thropologist. Specialists will argue with certain details
but cannot ignore this work. *After Kino: Jesuit Missions
in Northwestern New Spain, 1711-1767* by John A. Donohue,
S.J. (Rome, 1969) is a scholarly account of the Jesuit effort in the area evangelized by Father Eusebio Kino until
the suppression of the Society in Spain and the colonies in
1767. *Mission of Sorrows. Jesuit Guevavi and the Pimas, 1691-
1767* by John L. Kessell (Tucson, 1970) is a beautifully printed

volume, readable, admirably researched, and aptly illustrate
It tells the story of the daily rounds of the Jesuits at the
Guevavi mission, of the ferocity of the Apaches, of the de-
mise of the mission after the Society's suppression. *The
Spanish Borderlands Frontier, 1513-1821* by John ┆. Bannon,
S.J. (New York, 1970) gives a carefully nuanced picture of
the frontier meeting place of several cultural and political and religious influences in which the Jesuits had an
important role. Herbert Eugene Bolton, prince among pioneer historians of Spanish colonization in the west of
North America, gives a sympathetic and reliable picture
of Jesuit missionaries of the Mexican Province of the pre-
suppression Society in the fourth section of *Bolton and
the Spanish Borderlands*, edited by John F. Bannon, S.J.
(Norman, Oklahoma, 1964), a work in which Father Bannon
has assembled several essays of Bolton. In Section IV
there are three essays that treat the Jesuits, especially
the one entitled "The Black Robes of New Spain." One of
Bolton's most productive students, Peter Masten Dunne,
S.J., gives clear, scholarly accounts of Jesuit missionary
work in several works, each of whose titles indicates the
focus of the individual volume: *Pioneer Black Robes on the
West Coast 1591-1631* (Berkeley and Los Angeles, 1944);
Early Jesuit Missions in Tarahumara (Berkeley and Los
Angeles, 1948); *Black Robes in Lower California 1697-
1768* (Berkeley and Los Angeles, 1952). John F. Bannon,
S.J., presents a carefully detailed study of Jesuit work
in Sonora in his *The Mission Frontier in Sonora, 1620-
1687* (New York, 1955). The Jesuit period (1566-1572) takes
up most of *The Romance of the Floridas. The Finding and
the Founding* by Michael Kenny, S.J. (Milwaukee, 1934), a
work marred by inaccuracies and careless methodology. The
account of the murder of eight Spanish Jesuits in 1571 between the York and James rivers in present-day Virginia
is given in a volume superior in scholarship and rich in

details, *The Spanish Jesuit Mission in Virginia, 1570-1572*
by Clifford M. Lewis, S.J., and Albert J. Loomie, S.J.,
(Chapel Hill, 1953). *Educational Foundations of the Jesuits
in Sixteenth-Century New Spain* by Jerome V. Jacobsen, S.J.
(Berkeley, 1938) has as its purpose "to reveal the foundations of the Jesuit system of education in New Spain and
to describe its growth up to the opening of the seventeenth
century." In a scholarly, precise, and clear way Father
Jacobsen describes the Jesuit colleges in Mexico, from
Durango in the north to Oaxaca in the south, up to the
end of the 1500's.

D. North America: French Influence

The basic work for a knowledge of the Jesuits in New
France is the 73-volume set edited by Reuben Gold Thwaites,
*The Jesuit Relations and Allied Documents. Travels and Ex-
plorations of the Jesuit Missionaries in New France, 1610-
1791* (Cleveland, 1896-1901). A new edition in 39 volumes
appeared by use of photocopy process in New York in 1959.
An essential complement to this set is *Thwaites' Jesuit
Relations Errata and Addenda* by Joseph P. Donnelly, S.J.
(Chicago, 1967). *Black Gown and Redskins. Adventures and
Travels of the Early Jesuit Missionaries in North America
(1610-1791)*, edited by Edna Kenton (New York, 1956),
presents selections from Thwaites' edition of the *Jesuit
Relations*. Earlier editions of this volume appeared with
varying titles in London and New York. *The Jesuit Relations and Allied Documents: A Selection* **, edited by S.
R. Mealing (Toronto, The Carleton Library No. 7, 1963)
is one in "a series of Canadian reprints and new collections
of source material relating to Canada, issued under the
editorial supervision of the Institute of Canadian Studies,
Carleton University, Ottawa." *Saint Ignace: Canadian Altar*

of Martyrdom by William Sherwood Fox with the collabora-
tion of Wilfrid Jury (Toronto, 1949) is an illustrated account of the historical and archaeological background of
the village of St. Ignace. Much of the data in this work
is now seriously challenged by scholars. *The Excavation
of Ste. Marie I* by Kenneth E. Kidd (Toronto, 1949) is a
careful archaeological study with 50 plates of the old
Jesuit mission of Ste. Marie. *Frontenac and the Jesuits*
by Jean Delanglez, S.J. (Chicago, 1939) is a sound work
of scholarship that treats with calm the difficulties between the Society of Jesus and Louis de Buadé, Comte de
Frontenac, the royal governor of New France. It covers
carefully the three general problems: the brandy issue;
the alleged trading by the Jesuits; the methods of civil-
izing the Indians. *Jesuit and Savage in New France* by
John H. Kennedy (New Haven, 1950; reissued Hamden, Conn.,
1971) is a cogent, thorough, and objective work in which
the author shows that the literary type of the attractive
young heathen, with so little resemblance to the Red Indian,
picked up by the rationalists and the romanticists was in
large measure due to the reports of the Jesuits of New
France. Although the Jesuits drew grim pictures of the
savagery they met in New France, they also gave much space
in their reports to the Indians' natural virtues as good
foundations for the supernatural, so much in contrast with
the vices encountered among civilized Frenchmen at home,
and so unwittingly provided the rationalists and romanticists with arguments against dogma and law. Famous for
its literary grace and the warmth of appreciation for the
Jesuits by its Boston agnostic author is *The Jesuits in
North America in the Seventeenth Century* by Francis Park-
man (Boston, 1868). Reprinted several times, it appeared
as recently as 1963 in a new edition. *The French Jesuits
in Lower Louisiana* (1700-1963) by Jean Delanglez, S.J.
(Washington, 1935) is a carefully researched presentation

of the Jesuit side in the conflicts between the Society and the civil government and the Capuchins in Louisiana. Jesuits have a significant part in *Church and State in French Colonial Louisiana. Policy and Politics to 1732* by Charles Edwards O'Neill, S.J., (New Haven, 1966), a work of superior scholarship based on archival material in the United States, Canada, Great Britain, France, and Italy, and in which the author shows why the Louisianan "never attained the religious fervor of the Canadian." *Marquette's Explorations. The Narratives Re-examined* by Raphael N. Hamilton, S.J. (Madison, 1970) is an important, detective-like investigation of the authenticity of key documents in the story of Jacques Marquette, a study not undertaken even by the careful, earlier Marquette scholar, Jean Delanglez, S.J. This volume is a signal contribution to technical scholarship about the Jesuits in New France.

E. North America: English Influence

Thomas Hughes, S.J., in the Preface of the second volume of his *History of the Society of Jesus in North America. Colonial and Federal* (New York and London, 1907-1917) wrote the following: "In the growing settlements which were destined to become the United States of America, the history of Jesuits was that of the nascent Catholic Church." Hughes' work is therefore a history not only of the Jesuits but also of the origins of the Catholic Church within the first thirteen states of the United States of America. He therefore does not treat the Spanish settlements; nor the French except for that area that came under British rule after the peace of 1763. With sureness and steady command of wide-ranging documentation, Hughes in his magisterial work moves through more than a century, from the antecedents of the Maryland colony to the American

19

Revolution. He devotes two large volumes to narrative
and two equally large volumes to documentation. *The Ark
and the Dove: The Beginning of Civil and Religious Liberties in America* by J. Moss Ives (New York, 1936) is not
only a narrative account, readable though occasionally inaccurate, but also an exposition of the thesis that civil
and religious liberties enjoyed by Americans are due to
Maryland influence, especially that of John Carroll, Charles
Carroll of Carrollton, and Daniel Carroll. Edwin Warfield
Beitzell's *The Jesuit Missions of St. Mary's County, Maryland* (Washington, D.C., 1960) is local history at its best
by a man who knows the land, the people, and the Catholic
Church of Maryland's oldest colony. This volume, in type-
written form, covers 325 years, from Father Andrew White
to Father John LaFarge.

F. Asia

Donald F. Lach in his erudite and richly documented
Asia in the Making of Europe (Volume I in Book I and in
Book II, Chicago, 1965) devotes several chapters to Jesuit
missionary work in the Far East. This work with its ad-
mirable control of a wide range of source material is a
bibliographical goldmine. *Jesuits Go East* by Felix A.
Plattner, S.J., translated by Lord Sudley and Oscar Blobel
(Westminster, Md., 1952) is a readable, vivid, and broad
perspective of Jesuit endeavors in the Far East but is
marred by the absence of an index, an essential apparatus
in a book of this kind. Cornelius Wessels, S.J., in *Early
Jesuit Travellers in Central Asia, 1603-1721* (The Hague,
1924) gives scholarly and fascinating accounts of famous
Jesuit explorers such as Benito de Goes, Johann Grueber,
Francisco de Andrade, and others.

1. China

Generation of Giants. The Story of the Jesuits in China in the Last Decades of the Ming Dynasty by George H. Dunne, S.J. (Notre Dame, 1962) is a warmly sympathetic account in pungent and occasionally belligerent prose of the Jesuit enterprise in China until the death of Father Johann Adam Schall von Bell in 1666. *Missionary and Mandarin. The Jesuits at the Court of China* by Arnold H. Rowbotham (Berkeley and Los Angeles, 1942), a readable work, concentrates more on the cultural relations between Europe and China effected by the Jesuit missionaries rather than a recitation of the mission work itself. The author, because of insecure command of the sources, makes frequent mistakes. At once an indictment of the Congregation Propaganda Fide and an encomium of the Society's mission in China, *Failure in the Far East* by Malcolm Hay (Philadelphia, 1957), who writes with a chip on his shoulder, presents valuable research but suffers from an obviously polemical tone and intent. *Galileo in China. Relations through the Roman College between Galileo and the Jesuit Scientist-Missionaries (1610-1640)* by Pasquale M. D'Elia, S.J., translated by Rufus Suter and Matthew Sciascia (Cambridge, Mass., 1960) is a meticulously researched work by an outstanding authority on Father Matteo Ricci about a specialized corner of scientific history. Joseph Needham in his *Science and Civilization in China*, Volume III, *Mathematics and the Sciences of the Heavens and the Earth* (Cambridge, 1959) presents considerable material on Jesuit scientific work in China, contending that in some respects the Jesuits failed to appreciate ancient Chinese scientific data. Needham concentrates on the Jesuit-Chinese scientific relationships in his much shorter work, *Chinese Astronomy and the Jesuit Mission: An Encounter of Cultures* ** (London, 1958). J. B. Cummins in his excellent edition of *The*

V. Special Areas

Travels and Controversies of Friar Domingo Navarrete, (2 volumes, Cambridge, 1962) has a valuable introduction, in which he lucidly outlines some of the main facets of the Chinese Rites controversy, especially the acrimony between the Jesuits and the Dominicans. The latter had a most articulate spokesman in Friar Domingo Navarrete, one of whose polemical works is here edited. Superior scholarship and good organization characterize *The Jesuits and the Sino-Russian Treaty of Nerchinsk (1689). The Diary of Thomas Pereira, S.J.*, by Joseph Sebes, S.J., (Rome, 1961), in which the author describes the role of the Jesuits in the first treaty made between the Russians and the Chinese. Joseph Krahl, S.J., gives a vivid account of the last days of the Jesuit mission to China before the Society's suppression in his excellent *China Missions in Crisis: Bishop Laimbeckhoven and His Times 1738-1787* (Rome, 1964). The central figure is the great Austrian Jesuit and Bishop of Nanking, Gottfried Xaver von Laimbeckhoven. *Emperor of China* by Jonathan D. Spence (New York, 1974), an excellent "autobiographical biography," that is, a biography in which a skilled historian of China has interwoven his narrative with selections from the 16,000 pages of Emperor K'ang-hsi's writings, gives an insight into the mentality of the Chinese ruler who in the 17th and 18th centuries was the most open to the Jesuit missionaries. *The First Chinese Priest of the Society of Jesus. Emmanuel de Siqueira, 1633-1673 ***, *The Death of Stephen Faber, S.J., Apostle of Shensi, China ***, and *Maillard de Tournon, Papal Legate at the Court of Peking* by Francis A. Rouleau, S.J. are scholarly works which originally appeared as articles in *Archivum Historicum Societatis Iesu* between 1959 and 1962. *Jesuits Under Fire in the Siege of Hong Kong, 1941* by Thomas F. Ryan, S.J. (London, 1944) is a record compiled by Father Ryan from the individual experiences of several Jesuits during the siege that ended in the capture of Hong Kong by the Japanese during World War II. It is a vivid and absorbing narrative. *Wah Yan College, Hong Kong. Golden Jubilee 1919-1969*, no author given (Hong Kong, 1969), is a short account of the modern Jesuit intellectual enterprise in Hong Kong.

2. Japan

The best account of Jesuit success and failure in the 16th and 17th centuries in Japan is Charles R. Boxer's *The Christian Century in Japan, 1549-1650* (Berkeley, 1951), wherein Boxer gives, with a sure grasp of the vast source material, a balanced and thorough account of the Jesuit venture in Japan, the missionary principles of Father Alessandro Valignano, the contest between the Jesuits and the Franciscans about cultural accomodation, and the impact of the Dutch colonial expansion on the Catholic community. Jesuits appear prominently in *The Catholic Church in Japan* by Johannes Laures, S.J., (Tokyo, 1954), a small work, tightly packed with factual information and rather difficult for continuous reading. Michael Cooper, S.J., is the editor of *They Came to Japan. An Anthology of European Reports on Japan, 1543-1640* (Berkeley, 1965), in which the majority of the selections are from the correspondence and reports of Jesuit missionaries, including such famous men as Father Alessandro Valignano, Father Luis Froes, Father João Rodrigues. These selections, often vivdly written, are a tribute to the excellent reporting skill of the Jesuits. *The Southern Barbarians. The First Europeans in Japan*, edited by Michael Cooper, S.J. (Tokyo and Palo Alto, 1971), is a beautifully produced volume of 124 plates and five essays by distinguished scholars on the relations of the Japanese and those Europeans who entered Japan in the 16th and early 17th centuries. The Jesuits appear with great frequency. On their activity this volume throws much light in an urbane and sophisticated manner. *Kirishitan-ban no kenkyu. Studies of Books Printed by the Jesuit Mission Press in Japan* (Tenri, 1973) contains eight scholarly essays by different authors on various aspects, historical, technical, artistic, of the Jesuit printing enterprise in Japan. *Sophia University*

V. Special Areas

1913-1973. Sixtieth Anniversary of its Foundation **, author not given (Tokyo, 1973), is a brief and popular account of a major modern intellectual enterprise.

3. *India*

The Jesuits in Malabar (2 volumes, Bangalore, 1939 and 1951) and *The Jesuits in Mysore* (Kozhikode, 1955), both works by Domenico Ferroli, S.J., are replete with valuable material but disjointed in their narrative. Cardinal Eugène Tisserant provides a clear and well-organized account of the tragic story of the Malabar Christian community, in which Jesuits sometimes played laudable roles and sometimes ineffective and lamentable ones, in his *Eastern Christianity in India: A History of the Syro-Malabar Churc from the Earliest Time to the Present Day*, translated by E. R. Hambye, S.J. (Westminster, 1957). This work is a translation of Tisserant's article in the *Dictionnaire de théologie catholique:* Syro-Malabare (Église), Volume 14, Part 2. Edward MacLagan's *The Jesuits and the Great Mogul* (London, 1932) is a popular, highly dramatized and romanticized account of the Jesuit mission to the powerful Mogul at Fatehpur, Akbar, in the end of the sixteenth century, a mission whose first leader was Father Rodolfo Aquaviva, nephew of the famous Jesuit General, Claudio Aquaviva. *Jesuit Letters and Indian History 1542-1773* by John Correia-Afonso, S.J. (2nd edition, Bombay and London, 1969) is a meticulously researched doctoral thesis that purposes to evaluate Jesuit correspondence as a source for the historiography of India, and to give a general idea of the nature and contents of the letters. *Christianity in India. A History in Ecumenical Perspective*, edited by H. C. Perumalil, C.M.I. and E. R. Hambye, S.J. (Alleppey, India, 197 presents 12 essays by 9 authors on the history of the

Christian presence in India. Jesuits have an important
part in this volume, especially the missions to the Great
Mogul and in Madurai. Written by scholars for non-scholars,
this valuable work is difficult reading, aggravated by many
spelling mistakes and grammatical errors. Short histories
of some of the Jesuit schools in India give an insight into an important phase of the modern Jesuit effort there.
These include *St. Francis Xavier's Apostolic School, Madurai.
Golden Jubilee Souvenir 1918-1968*, author not given (Madurai,
1968); *St. Joseph's College Tiruchirapalli. Platinum Jubilee,
1896-1971* author not given (Tiruchirapalli, 1971); *St. Xavier's
Institute of Education. 10th Anniversary*, no author given
(Bombay, 1963).

4. *The Philippine Islands*

The Jesuits in the Philippines, 1581-1768 by Horacio
de la Costa, S.J. (Cambridge, Mass., 1961) is not only a
work of superior scholarship but one that is skillfully
and gracefully written. A second volume is anticipated
to carry the story to the modern age.

G. *Canada after 1763*

The Treaty of Paris (1763) placed Canada under the
English crown, terminating the long dominion by France.
*The Jesuits' Estates Question, 1760-1888. A Study of the
Background for the Agitation of 1889* by Roy C. Dalton
(Toronto, 1968) is a well documented and intriguing study
of complicated background of the political row over the
disposition of the lands of the old Jesuit misisons.
Loyola and Montreal by Timothy P. Slattery (Montreal,
1962) is a popular and rather thin recital that focuses
on the Jesuit presence in Montreal since the arrival of

6 Jesuits in that city in 1842, with special emphasis on
the creation and growth of Loyola College.

H. Europe

*Rome and the Counter-Reformation in Scandinavia, 1539-
1583* by Oskar Garstein (Oslo, 1964) has as its focal point
a clear and carefully documented account of the Jesuits'
abortive effort to unite the 16th century Sweden of John
III to the Catholic Church. It vividly portrays the issues, liturgical and disciplinary, on which the Jesuit
enterprise splintered. *Records of the English Province
of the Society of Jesus*, edited by Henry Foley, S.J. (8
volumes, London, 1877-1882) "is not intended to be a for-
mal history, exactly and chronologically arranged, but
simply a record of the labours and sufferings of the members of the English Province S.J. in the propagation and
preservation of the faith of our ancestors, during the
most eventful and exciting times of its existence." This
work is therefore a valuable but disjointed mixture of
narrative and documentation about the English Jesuits
through the 16th and 17th centuries. *The English Jesuits.
From Campion to Martindale* by Bernard Basset, S.J. (New
York, 1968) is a popular, readable, entertaining, chatty
survey of the Society in English history. Father Basset
gives special emphasis to anecdotes about and portraits
of individual Jesuits. *The Jesuits and the Popish Plot*
by Malcolm V. Hay (London, 1934) reveals Hay's peculiar
instinct for detective work as he unfolds the careless
use of documents by even eminent historians in the famous
case of Titus Oates and his bogus efforts to implicate the
Jesuits in an alleged plot against the Crown in 1678. This
work demands of the reader considerable concentration on
the unfolding of historical evidence. *The Popish Plot* by

John Kenyon (London, 1972) is a balanced presentation of
the impact that the Titus Oates story had on the government, politics, the Catholic community. Eleven Jesuits,
including the provincial, Father Thomas Whitebread, were
executed because of the Oates' lie. Blessed Claude de la
Colombière, chaplain to the Duchess of York, was imprisoned.
Clongowes Record by Timothy Corcoran, S.J. (Dublin, 1932)
contains a brief but informative sketch of the Jesuit experience in Ireland by a careful scholar. *The Irish Jesuits
1560-1814*, edited by J. B. Stephenson, S.J. (Dublin, 1962),
is a collection of articles on the history of the Irish
Province taken from various sources, especially the Jesuit
Year Book. This collection is in type-written form and is
circulated privately. *Memoirs of Scottish Catholics during the XVII and XVIII Centuries* by William Forbes-Leith,
S.J. (2 volumes, London and New York, 1909) is a clear,
interesting, straightforward narrative, close to the sources,
about the Society's uncertain days in Scotland. *St. Omers
to Stonyhurst* by Hubert Chadwick, S.J. (London, 1962) is
an informative, interesting, and scholarly account of the
educational venture of the English Jesuits that started
in St. Omers in 1593 and continued through two centuries
through Bruges, Liège, and Stonyhurst, where the college
settled in 1794. *Guy Fawkes--The Real Story of the Gunpowder Plot?* by Francis Edwards, S.J. (London, 1969) is
a valuable, critical, minute re-examination of a famous
episode in English history into which some Jesuits were
swept. It seriously challenges the "official" version of
the Gunpowder Plot that has held the field through the
centuries. *Henry III and the Jesuit Politicians* by A.
Lynn Martin (Geneva, 1973) is a carefully researched and
readable inquiry into the diplomatic and political activity
of French Jesuits during the critical period 1570-1590.
The author focuses his attention on three, Fathers Emond
Auger, Claude Matthieu, and Henri Samier, and concludes

that the French Jesuits who engaged in politics were few,
and that these few failed in obedience to the Jesuit General, Claudio Aquaviva. The *Jansenists and the Expulsion
of the Jesuits from France, 1757-1765* by Dale Van Kley
(New Haven, 1975) is basically a doctoral thesis which
judges that the destruction of the Society in France was
due to a small but effective group of Jansenists in the
Paris *Parlement,* who used the financial disaster of Jesuit
Antoine La Valette as a weapon against the Society. The
author used several archives in France but seemingly did
not consult archives in Rome. *Colleges in Controversy.
The Jesuit Schools in France from Revival to Suppression,
1815-1880* by John W. Padberg, S.J. (Cambridge, Mass., 1969),
a work of scholarly skill and objectivity that is based
almost exclusively on previously unused archival documentation, places the Jesuit schools of 19th century France
against the background of anti-clericalism, revolution,
swift shifts of government up to the early years of the
Third Republic. *The Jesuits in Poland. The Lothian Essay,
1892* by A. F. Pollard (New York, 1971 reprint) was first
published in 1892 by a famous historian of Jesus College,
Oxford, and advances the thesis that Poland's decline was
in large measure due to Jesuit failure to take positive
measure to save the country.

I. The United States

The Jesuits of the Middle United States by Gilbert J.
Garraghan, S.J. (3 volumes New York, 1938) is a reliable
and thorough study of the origins, growth, and expansion
of the Jesuits in Mid-America, their works among the
Indians, on the frontier, and in the schools. Abundant
quotations from original documents give a genuine feel
for this arduous era in American Jesuit history. Father
Garraghan supplies many excellent maps and photographs.

The Return of the Jesuits Francis X. Curran, S.J. (Chicago, 1966) is a collection of seven scholarly and well-written articles on the establishment of the Jesuits within different areas of the United States and Canada. It covers the Jesuit apostolate in New York City, Western New York State, Kentucky, Canada, and the push of the German Jesuits from Buffalo to South Dakota and Wyoming. *A Report on the American Jesuits* by Margaret Bourke-White and John La Farge, S.J. (New York, 1956) is an attractive amalgam of Ms. Bourke-White's excellent photography and Father La Farge's smooth, intelligent commentary on the American Jesuits at the threshold of Vatican Council II. *Old Jesuit Trails in Penn's Forest* by Leo G. Fink (New York, 1933) is a popular and occasionally inaccurate account of the Jesuit apostolate in eastern Pennsylvania. The earlier chapters cover the pre-Suppression Jesuits in Penn's colony. *The Jesuits in Old Oregon* by William N. Bischoff, S.J. (Caldwell, Idaho, 1945), a brief and clear account of the Jesuits in the Northwest, including several of the colorful Italians, has a valuable biographical index of the missionaries. *The Jesuits and the Indian Wars of the Northwest* by Robert I. Burns, S.J. (New Haven, 1966), a scholarly work of great importance for an understanding of American history in the Oregon Territory, won for Father Burns the John Gilmary Shea prize. *Jesuits in Montana 1840-1860* ** by Wilfred P. Schoenberg, S.J. (Portland, Ore., 1960), an attractive pamphlet of 120 pages, is a popular and clear recital of almost 100 years of Jesuit work among the Flatheads, the Pend d'Oreilles, the Blackfeet, the Gros Ventres, and other Indian tribes. Fr. Schoenberg is also the author of other works that give in broad outline the apostolate of the Jesuits in the Northwest: *A Chronicle of the Catholic History of the Pacific Northwest: 1743-1960* (Portland, Oregon, 1960) and *Jesuits in Oregon: 1844-1959* (Portland, Oregon, 1960).

V. Special Areas

The Nez Perce Indians and the Opening of the Northwest by
Alvin M. Josephy, Jr. (New Haven, 1965) is an excellent
work in which appear succinctly such famous Jesuits as
De Smet, Cataldo, Gazzoli, Joset, Mengarini, Point, Ravalli.
Jesuit labor at the other end of the United States, in
Maine, is related in a precise and scholarly way in *Catholic Church in Maine* by William L. Lucey, S.J. (Frances-
town, New Hampshire, 1957). Local studies about Jesuit
work in the central states are abundant. The early history of Jesuit involvement in Kansas and its frontiers is
told in scholarly detail in *The Jesuits in Territorial
Kansas, 1827-1861. A Contribution to the Centennial of the
Statehood of Kansas* by Augustine C. Wand, S.J. (St. Marys,
Kansas, 1962). Fr. Gilbert Garraghan, S.J., is the author
of several short works, all done with his careful scholarship and clear narrative: *The Catholic Church in Chicago,
1673-1871* (Chicago, 1921); *Catholic Beginnings in Kansas
City, Missouri* (Chicago, 1920); *St. Ferdinand de Floris-
sant: The Story of an Ancient Parish* (Chicago, 1923); *Chapters in Frontier History: Research Studies in the Making
of the West* (Milwaukee, 1934). Jesuits have a significant
role in each of Fr. Garraghan's titles. *The Holy Family
Parish, Chicago: Priests and People* by Thomas Mulkerins
(Chicago, 1923) is a popular and informative description
of the Jesuit parish that was the most vibrant in the
early history of Chicago. *Journal* by Christian Hoecken,
S.J. (St. Marys, Kansas, 1890) is an excellent first-hand
description of Jesuit work among the Kaw, the Sioux, the
Potawatomi, the Kickapoo. Fr. Hoecken was an outstanding
missionary priest. *Jesuit Missions Among the Sioux* by
Louis Goll, S.J., (St. Francis Mission, S.D., 1940) is a
brief and popular account in the area suggested by the
title. *The Holy See and the Nascent Church in the Middle
Western United States, 1820-1850* by Robert F. Trisco (Rome,
1962) is an important scholarly contribution to the under-

30

standing of the Church's origins in that area, in which
the Jesuits had a significant role. *Jesuit beginnings in
New Mexico* by Sister Lilliana Owens (El Paso, 1950) is a
sketch in broad lines of the Italian Jesuit mission created
at the invitation of Archbishop Lamy of Santa Fe. It contains interesting quotations from Father Donato Gasparri's
account of the trek to New Mexico in 1867 and from Father
Livio Vigilante's diary of the Mission of New Mexico, 1867-
1874. *The Jesuits in New Orleans and the Mississippi Valley* by Albert Biever, S.J. (New Orleans, 1924) is a small,
rapid outline, almost in chronicle fashion, of the Jesuit
experience in the Cresent City and the Mississippi environs
through the 1800's and early 1900's, preceded by a short
survey of pre-Suppression happenings. *American Jesuits*
by James J. Walsh (New York, 1934) is a superficial and
uncritical work whose title is inaccurate. It rambles
through 19 chapters on such subjects as "Jesuit War Chaplains," "Alaska Missions," "United States Chief Justices
and Jesuit Friends." *Jesuits for the Negro* by Edward D.
Reynolds, S.J. (New York, 1949) tells in popular and
anecdotal style the history of Jesuit work among the Blacks
of the United States, a story which, except for the 300
years in Maryland, was not a wide and organized apostolate
but rather "a series of skirmishes with the problem of
bringing the colored people into the Catholic Church." Although based on the wide bibliography (some 25,000 cards
and 500,000 entries) of Arnold Garvey, S.J., this volume
is not scholarly and has no index. *Dogsled Apostles* by
A. H. Savage (New York, 1942) is a popular, pietistic, and
romanticized account of the Jesuit missions in Alaska, the
central figure being Bishop Joseph Crimont, S.J., who
labored in Alaska for 51 years. Another popular account
of the Alaskan Mission is given in *Jesuits in Alaska* by
Segundo Llorente, S.J. (Portland, Oregon, 1969).

A great deal of American Jesuit history is contained

in works about the universities and colleges staffed by the
Society of Jesus. Not all the 28 universities and colleges
have published their individual histories. Some have them in
manuscript form. Following are the published works. *A History
of Boston College* by David R. Dunigan, S.J. (Milwaukee,
1947); *Canisius College: The First Hundred Years* by Charles
A. Brady (Buffalo, 1969) and *Canisius College. The First
Nine Years, 1870-1879* by Thomas E. Harney (New York, 1971);
*Creighton University: Reminiscences of the First Twenty-
Five Years* by M. P. Dowling, S.J. (Omaha, 1903); *Up to the
Present. The Story of Fordham* by Robert I. Gannon, S.J.
(New York, 1967); *Georgetown University: Origin and Early
Years* by John M. Daley, S.J. (Washington, 1957) and *George-
town University: The Middle Years: 1840-1900* by Joseph T.
Durkin, S.J. (Washington, 1963); *Gonzaga University;
Seventy-Five Years 1887-1962* by W. P. Shoenberg, S.J.
(Spokane, 1963); *The Spires of Fenwick: A History of the
College of the Holy Cross, 1843-1963* by Walter J. Meagher,
S.J., and William J. Grattan (New York, 1966); *Historical
Sketch of Loyola College, Baltimore, 1852-1902* by J. J.
Ryan, S.J. (Baltimore, 1903); *The Story of Marquette
University* by Raphael N. Hamilton, S.J. (Milwaukee, 1953);
*Jesuit Education in Philadelphia, Saint Joseph's College,
1851-1926* by Francis X. Talbot, S.J. (Philadelphia, 1927);
*Historical Sketch of St. Louis University: The Celebration
of Its Fiftieth Anniversary, June 24, 1879* by Walter H.
Hill, S.J. (St. Louis, 1879); *Better the Dream. St. Louis
University and Community, 1818-1968* by William B. Faherty,
S.J. (St. Louis, 1968); *Catholic Culture in Alabama. Cen-
tenary Study of Spring Hill College 1830-1930* by Michael
Kenny, S.J. (New York, 1931); *University of Santa Clara:
A History, 1777-1912* by J. P. Morrissey (Santa Clara, 1912)
and *The History of Santa Clara College. A Study of Jesuit
Education in California, 1851-1912* by Gerald McKevitt, S.J.
(Los Angeles, 1972); *The First Half Century of St. Ignatius*

Church and College by J. W. Riordan, S.J. (San Francisco, 1905) and *Jesuits by the Golden Gate. The Society of Jesus in San Francisco, 1849-1969* by John B. McGloin, S.J. (San Francisco, 1972).

A.   St. Ignatius

There is no completely satisfactory biography of St.
Ignatius that keeps a balance between his exterior life
and his interior life and that is abreast of recent Ignatian research.   Among the better narrative accounts of Ignatius' life are those by two non-Catholics, Paul Van Dyke,
author of *Ignatius Loyola* (New York, 1926), and Henry D.
Sedgwick, author of *Ignatius Loyola* (New York, 1923).   Of
these works James Brodrick, S.J., writes: "The two books
are easily the fairest Protestant accounts of Ignatius ever
written, and, as history, are far superior to many Catholic
accounts."   Mary Purcell's *The First Jesuit* * (Westminster,
Md., 1957) is generally dependable and in an easy narrative
style.   A small but authoritative work, *A Short Life of St.
Ignatius Loyola*, translated by Robert Hull, S.J. (Bombay,
1955), is by the author of the magisterial work on the
Spanish Assistancy, Antonio Astráin, S.J.   *St. Ignatius
Loyola* by Francis Thompson (Baltimore, 1951), frequently
re-issued, is written in a romantic vein and is flawed by
historical errors.   *St. Ignatius of Loyola* by Paul Dudon,
S.J.,   translated by William J. Young, S.J. (Milwaukee,
1949), is the most scholarly, extensive, and reliable biography in English but it is quite dense in parts, especially
in the beginning, because of the large amount of background
details.   Dudon's use of excessively pious expressions also
jars.   Giorgio Papasogli's *Saint Ignatius of Loyola*, translated by Paul Garvin (New York, 1960), appeared originally
in Italian and is a simple, straightforward account.   The
first of James Brodrick's projected two-volume life of St.
Ignatius is *Saint Ignatius Loyola. The Pilgrim Years* (New
York, 1956).   This pleasantly written work is especially
rich in its picture of the cultural and social background
within which Ignatius lived.   It takes the story only to

34

1538, before the confirmation of the Society. Father
Brodrick died before finishing the second volume. One of
the greatest modern authorities on St. Ignatius, Pedro de
Leturia, S.J., is the author of *Iñigo de Loyola*, translated by Aloysius Owen, S.J. (Syracuse, 1949), which,
while not easy reading, is most helpful in tracing the
formative influences in the saint's character and the literary traditions expressed in his spiritual writings.
Leonard von Matt, as photographer, and Hugo Rahner, S.J.,
as narrator, have produced a beautiful volume in *St. Ignatius Loyola: A Pictorial Biography* * (Chicago, 1956). In
his superior *Saint Ignatius Loyola. Letters to Women*, translated by Kathleen Pond and S.A.H. Weetman (New York, 1960),
Hugo Rahner, S.J., presents all the surviving correspondence
that Ignatius had with women, 139 letters, the 89 he wrote
and the 50 he received. Rahner divides the women with whom
Ignatius corresponded into several classes: Royal Ladies,
Noble Ladies, Benefactresses, Spiritual Daughters, Mothers
of Fellow-Jesuits, Friends. He presents each letter within
the historical and social context of the period. These
analyses, with the General Introduction, constitute probably the best study of the human qualities of St. Ignatius.
Toward the end of his life St. Ignatius dictated a short
autobiography. He carried it to only 1538, except for a
few remarks about his later years. This is an indispensable
document for an understanding of the saint's interior life.
There are two English editions that are based on the original Spanish-Italian. The more recent is *The Autobiography of St. Ignatius Loyola* **, translated by Joseph F.
O'Callaghan and edited by John C. Olin (New York, 1974).
This is in the Torchbooks Series of Harper & Row. The
earlier edition is *St. Ignatius' Own Story as Told to Luis
Gonzalez de Camara*, edited and translated by William J.
Young, S.J. (Chicago, 1956). With this edition are in-
cluded eleven selected letters of St. Ignatius. William

VI. Biographies

J. Young, S.J., edits and translates 228 letters of St.
Ignatius in *Letters of St. Ignatius of Loyola* (Chicago,
1959). St. Ignatius of Loyola, *The Constitutions of the
Society of Jesus: Translated, with an Introduction and a Commentary*, by George E. Ganss, S.J. (St. Louis, 1970), is now
the basic tool in English for a genuine understanding of
St. Ignatius' conception of the Society of Jesus. Father
Ganss' book includes the Formula of the Institute as well
as the *General Examen*, the *Constitutions*, and their *Declara-
tions*; and notes are full, comprehensive, and most helpful
in illuminating the *Constitutions* within their historical
context. *Ignatius the Theologian* by Hugo Rahner, S.J.,
translated by Michael Barry (New York, 1968), presents a
masterful appreciation of St. Ignatius' personal spiritual
endowments, experiences, and teaching as expressed in the
Spiritual Exercises, the discernment of spirits, the application of the senses, and his sensitivity to the authority of the Church. *The Spirituality of St. Ignatius
Loyola* by Hugo Rahner, S.J., translated by Francis J. Smith,
S.J. (Westminster, Md., 1953), is a penetrating historical
study of how "the spirit of service in the Church" found
realization in the life of St. Ignatius. *The Spiritual
Exercises of St. Ignatius*, translated by Louis J. Puhl,
S.J. (Westminster, Md., 1957), aims "to represent as nearly
as possible, idea with idea, Spanish idiom with correspond-
ing English idiom, Spanish sentence structure with English
sentence structure, and the quaint forms of the original
with the forms common at present" of a key document for an
understanding of St. Ignatius' interior spirit. English
translations of the *Spiritual Exercises* and English com-
mentaries on them are abundant. *The Ignatian Way to God*
by Alexandre Brou, S.J., translated by William J. Young,
S.J. (Milwaukee, 1952), and *Ignatian Methods of Prayer* by
Alexandre Brou, S.J., translated by William J. Young, S.J.
(Milwaukee, 1949), are lucid expositions, supported by ample

quotations, of one facet of St. Ignatius' ascetical and mystical life.

B. *General Collections*

The Fifth Week by William J. O'Malley, S.J. (Chicago, 1976) is a lively, vividly and engagingly written work in three parts. In the first Fr. O'Malley presents vignettes of Jesuits of the Past; in the second, vignettes of Jesuits of the Present, including the interesting development of his own vocation; and in the third, Jesuits of the Future, a description of the challenges a late 20th century Jesuit will probably face. *Wings of Eagles* by Francis J. Corley, S.J., and Robert J. Willmes, S.J. (Milwaukee, 1941) is a collection of 42 essays, each 3 to 6 pages in length, on the saints and the beatified of the Society. The authors aimed to present "original and accurate narratives, graphic, colorful, dramatic . . ." The style is popular and occasionally pietistic. *Jesuits*, edited by Robert Nash, S.J. (Westminster, Md., 1956), is a set of 19 vignettes of Jesuits of different countries and centuries, including St. Aloysius Gonzaga, Archbishop Alban Goodier, Joseph de Guibert, Pierre Charles, Daniel Lord. *Companions of Jesus. Spiritual Profiles of the Jesuit Saints and Beati* **, edited by Hugh Kay (London, 1974), presents in 37 short essays by different authors the "spiritual profiles" of the Society's 37 canonized saints and 134 beatified. The purpose of these essays is to stress "the salient characteristics of the personal spiritual life" of these Jesuits against their historical background. The essays run about 4 pages each; are, in several instances, translated from foreign languages; vary in quality, some being markedly preachy in tone. A list of the saints and beatified concludes this volume of 159 pages.

VI.   Biographies

C.   Pre-suppression

1.   Asia and Africa

St. Francis Xavier, Apostle of the East by Margaret
Yeo (London, 1931) is a thin and romanticized picture of
Francis. *Saint Francis Xavier (1506-1552)* by James Brodrick, S.J. (New York, 1952) is perhaps the least successful of Father Brodrick's several biographies of Jesuits.
The style is apposite but several factual errors mar the
work.   Father Brodrick's occasional cavalier attitude
toward Eastern religions can have a jarring effect on the
reader. *Life of St. Francis Xavier, Evangelist, Explorer,
Mystic* by Edith Anne Steward (London, 1917) receives high
praise from James Brodrick, S.J., who in 1940 judged that
this work, "except for occasional small ebullitions of
Protestant sentiment, is more scholarly and satisfying
than any English Catholic biography of the saint."   Ms.
Stewart's volume must yield this honor to the monumental
work of Georg Schurhammer, S.J.   The most thorough and accurate of all the biographies of St. Francis Xavier is
Francis Xavier. His Life, His Times.   Volume I *Europe (1506-
1541)*, translated by M. Joseph Costelloe, S.J. (Rome, 1973)
This volume of 791 pages is the first of four done in German by Schurhammer and takes Francis to 1541 and his de-
parture from Lisbon for the Indies.   Pedro de Leturia,
S.J., and Hugo Rahner, S.J., both superior Ignatian scholars
describe this volume as the definitive history of the origins of the Society of Jesus.   Because of the encyclopedic
collection of details, the person of Francis is sometimes
obscured, and reading can be difficult.   Vincent Cronin,
with learning and a graceful style, gives convincing accounts of the Society's early efforts in meeting the need
for cultural adaptation in the missionary thrust into the
Far East in a life of Matteo Ricci, S.J., *The Wise Man from*

the West * (New York, 1955), and in a life of Roberto de
Nobili, S.J., *A Pearl to India* (New York, 1959). De
Nobili is the subject of three important works by Fr. S.
Rajamanickam, S.J. The first is the author's doctoral
thesis on de Nobili as a literary figure, *The First Ori-
ental Scholar. Robert de Nobili, alias Tattuva Podagar, the
Father of Tamil Prose* (Tirunelveli, 1972). The second and
third works are English translations of two of de Nobili's
important works: *On Indian Customs* (Palayamkottai, 1972)
and *Adaptation* (Palayamkottai, 1971). These translations
make available to readers of English de Nobili's personal
expression of his principles for Christian cultural adaptation. *China in the Sixteenth Century: The Journals of
Matteo Ricci: 1583-1610* by Louis Gallagher, S.J., (New
York, 1953) is the English version of a Latin work edited
by Nicolas Trigault, S.J., one of Ricci's closest collabora-
tors in China. *Adam Schall. A Jesuit at the Court of China
1592-1666,* translated and adapted by Rachel Attwater (Milwaukee, 1963), tells in an easy style the story of the influential Jesuit from Cologne. This work is based on the
original French volume by Joseph Duhr, S.J. *Garlic for
Pegasus: The Life of Brother Benito de Goes* by Wilfred
P. Shoenberg, S.J. (Westminster, Md., 1955) tells in popular style the story of the Jesuit brother who crossed
"the roof of the world" from India to China in search of
Christians supposed to inhabit mysterious Cathay. *Life of
Venerable Gonçalo de Silveira* by Hubert Chadwick, S.J.
(New York, 1910) is a brief and clearly narrated account
of the first Jesuit to penetrate the area of the Zambesi
River, where in 1560 he was murdered. *Gonçalo da Silveira***
by W. F. Rea, S.J. (Salisbury, Rhodesia, 1960) is a short
work of 42 pages, which depends basically on the same
sources as the previous title. *A Gallant Conquistador* by
Donal Donnelly, S.J. (London, 1932) is a clear, smooth-
running narrative of Father Rodolfo Aquaviva's mission to

the Great Mogul in the second half of the 16th century.
It is generally solidly based on the sources, although
the author indulges in occasional imaginative passages.
Aquaviva and the Great Mogul by J. Stephen Narayan (Patna,
1945) is a sharp and straightforward account of the Aquaviva mission, in which the author relies greatly on the
Commentarius of Father Antonio de Monserrate, Aquaviva's
companion. *Giuseppe Castiglione. A Jesuit Painter at the
Court of the Chinese Emperors* by Cécile and Michel Beurdeley,
translated by Michael Bullock (Rutland, Vermont, 1971), is
a beautiful volume containing reproductions of the fascinating paintings of the Italian Jesuit brother who worked
at the court of Peking under three emperors in the 18th
century. The authors provide a sketch of Castiglione's
life as well as an informed critique of his artistic gifts
and his influence in China. *Rhodes of Viet Nam. The Travels
and Missions of Father Alexander de Rhodes in China and
Other Kingdoms of the Orient,* translated by Solange Hertz
(Westminster, Md., 1966) is a personal account by one of
the more original missionaries of the Society in the 17th
century. *A Prisoner in Japan. Carlo Spinola, S.J.* by Donal
Donnelly, S.J. tells in an uncritical and romanticized way
the story of one of the Jesuits martyred in Japan in the 17th
century. *Rodrigues the Interpreter: An Early Jesuit in
Japan and China* by Michael Cooper, S.J. (New York and Tokyo,
1974) relates in an absorbing way the story of the influential Portuguese Jesuit, João Rodrigues Tcuzzi, who was
at home with all classes in Japan during the intricate
Luso-Japanese contacts during the late 16th century and
the early 1600s. This volume is handsomely produced and
illustrated. Another excellent work by Father Cooper on
João Rodrigues Tcuzzi is his edition and translation of
*This Island of Japan. João Rodrigues' Account of 16th Cen-
tury Japan* (Tokyo, 1974), which received the Japan Broad-
casting Corporation Award in 1974. *Red Sand. A Life of*

St. John de Brito, S.J. Martyr of the Madura Mission by
A. Saulière, S.J. (Madura, 1947), written in a romantic
style, is directed primarily to younger readers.

2. *The Americas*

a. *Areas of Spanish and Portuguese Influence*

Peter Claver. Saint of the Slaves by Angel Valtierra,
S.J., translated by Janet H. Perry and L. J. Woodward (Westminster, Md., 1960) is about the saint who, as interpreted
by James Brodrick, S.J., was a fusion of the Curé d'Ars,
St. Francis Xavier, and Father Damian of Molokai. Even
though Valtierra aims to clear away the many legends from
the truth, and tries to make judicious use of the many
sources, St. Peter emerges as a somewhat enigmatic person.
In his *A Saint in the Slave Trade* (London, 1935) Arnold
Lunn gives a distractingly large treatment of the mechanics
of the slave trade to the detriment of picturing the person
of St. Peter. *What Are Saints?* by C. C. Martindale, S.J.,
(London, 1937) includes a perceptive appreciation of St.
Peter Claver's psychology. *Apostle of Brazil* by Helen
Dominion (New York, 1958) is a substantial work consider-
ably packed with background material about Father José
Anchieta, who arrived in Brazil in 1553 and spent forty-
four years there and who distinguished his missionary life
as a superior linguist and catechist. In his lecture *A
Great Luso-Brazilian Figure, Padre Antonio Vieira, S.J.,
1608-1697* ** (London, 1957), Charles R. Boxer with his characteristic scholarship and lucidity gives a fine portrait
of the great Portuguese missionary who helped by his elo-
quence to mould the modern Portuguese language. *Rim of
Christendom* by Herbert E. Bolton (New York, 1936) is a beautifully told story by a superior scholar of the great

cartographer, diarist, explorer, and missionary of Lower
California, Pimería Alta, and Arizona, Father Eusebio Kino.
*The Padre on Horseback. A Sketch of Eusebio Francisco Kino,
S.J., Apostle of the Pimas* (San Francisco, 1932) is Bolton's
very brief outline of the Kino story. This work was reissued in the American West Reprint Series in 1963 by Loyola
University Press, Chicago, with John F. Bannon, S.J., doing
the editing. Bolton also translated and edited *Kino's Historical Memoir of Pimería Alta* (2 volumes, Cleveland, 1919).
Pioneer Padre. The Life and Times of Eusebio Francisco Kino
by Rufus Wyllys (Dallas, 1935) is a detailed, colorful, and
graphic portrayal of Kino the man against the background
in which he worked. *A Kino Guide* ** by Charles Polzer,
S.J. (Tucson, 1972) is a popular account, with no loss of
scholarly accuracy, of the wide travels of Father Kino.
Maps and pictures enhance this attractive guide to Kino
missions and monuments. *Father Kino in Arizona* by Fay Jackson Smith, John L. Kessell and Francis J. Fox, S.J. (Phoe-
nix, 1966) is a handsome volume that presents in English
for the first time Kino's *Relación Diaria,* new information
about Kino's part in the settlement of the Guevavi and Tu-
macaori, and finally a selective bibliography about Kino.
*Kino and Manje. Explorers of Sonora and Arizona. Their
Vision of the Future. A Study of Their Expeditions and
Plans* by Ernest Burrus, S.J. (Rome, 1971) is a long, meticulously documented account of the exploring activities of
Father Kino and Juan Mateo Mange. *Kino's Biography of
Francisco Javier Saeta, S.J.,* edited by Ernest Burrus, S.J.,
and translated by Charles Polzer, S.J. (Rome, 1971) is Kino's
account of a Jesuit fellow missionary who was slain by na-
tives in 1695. *Kino and the Cartography of Northwestern
New Spain* by Ernest J. Burrus, S.J., (Tucson, 1965) is a
precise scholarly account of one aspect of Kino's great
talents. Father Burrus edits several documents of Kino in
Kino Reports to Headquarters. Correspondence of Eusebio F.

Kino, S.J. from New Spain with Rome (Rome, 1954); *Kino Writes to the Duchess. Letters of Eusebio Francisco Kino, S.J. to the Duchess of Aveiro* (Rome, 1965); *Kino's Plan for the Development of Pimería Alta, Arizona, and Upper California. A Report to the Mexican Viceroy* (Tucson, 1961). Father Burrus, besides his work on Kino, edits the documents of other Jesuits of the pre-suppression Mexican Province in *Ducrue's Account of the Expulsion of the Jesuits from Lower California (1767-1769)* (Rome, 1967), in *Wenceslaus Linck's Diary of His 1766 Expedition to Northern Baja California* (Los Angeles, 1966), and in *Wenceslaus Linck's Reports and Letters, 1762-1778* (Los Angeles, 1967). *Missionary in Sonora. The Travel Reports of Joseph Och, S.J., 1755-1767* by Theodore Treutlein (San Francisco, 1965) throws valuable light on Jesuit work in Sonora. *Gonzalo de Tapia* by W. Eugene Shiels, S.J. (New York, 1934) is a brief and scholarly account of one of the greater Jesuit missionaries in 16th-century Mexico, who was murdered by the Indians in 1594. Father Peter Masten Dunne, S.J., contributes richly detailed pictures of the Sonora-Arizona scene in three works that combine biography and editing of new texts: *Andrés Pérez de Ribas, Pioneer Black Robe of the West Coast, Administrator, Historian* (New York, 1951); *Jacobo Sedelmayr, Missionary, Frontiersman, Explorer in Arizona and Sonora. Four Original Manuscript Narratives, 1744-1751.* (Tucson, 1955); *Juan Antonio Balthasar, Padre Visitador to the Sonora Frontier, 1744-1745. Two Original Reports* (Tucson, 1957). Theodore E. Treutlein edits and translates a work of Father Ignaz Pfefferkorn, one of the many German-speaking Jesuits who went to Sonora-Arizona, in *Sonora. A Description of a Province* (Albuquerque, 1949). One of the more valuable Jesuit reports on Lower California is that of the Alsatian Jesuit, Johann Jakob Baegert, who labored in Lower California for 17 years until the suppression of the Society. On his return to Europe he wrote *Nachrichten*

von der Amerikanischen Halbinsel Californien. N. M. Branden
burg and Carl L. Baumann translate this in *Observation in
Lower California* (Berkeley and Los Angeles, 1952). *Life
and Works of the Reverend Ferdinand Konšćak, S.J. 1703-
1759,* author unknown, (Boston, 1923) is a valuable selection from the correspondence and diary of a Croatian Jesuit
who labored in Lower California. A more recent work on
Fr. Konšćak is *The Apostolic Life of Fernando Consag, Explorer of Lower California* by Francisco Zevallos, S.J.,
edited and translated by Manuel P. Servin (Los Angeles,
1968), who believes that Fr. Consag was "the greatest
Jesuit explorer in the Peninsula." *Juan Maria de Salva-
tierra, S.J. Selected Letters about Lower California,*
edited and translated by Ernest Burrus, S.J. (Los Angeles,
1971) throws valuable light on one of the greater Jesuits
who worked in Lower California. *The Cora Indians of Baja
California. The Relación of Father Ignacio Maria Napoli,
S.J.,* edited and translated by James Robert Moriarty III
and Benjamin F. Smith (Los Angeles, 1970) gives the almost
poetic account of the fertility of the land at Las Palmas
Bay by the first missionary to work among the Cora Indians
in the lower regions of Baja California. *The Drawings of
Ignacio Tirsch. A Jesuit Missionary in Baja California,*
narrative by Doyce B. Nunis, Jr. and translated by Elisa-
beth Schulz-Bischof (Los Angeles, 1972) is made up mainly
of 47 drawings by a Czech Jesuit while in Baja California
during the 1760s. These paintings by a talented amateur
are among the best known illustrations of Baja California
by an artist who lived there.

b. *Areas of French Influence*

Francis X. Talbot, S.J., is the author of *Saint Among
Savages: The Life of Isaac Jogues* * (New York, 1935) and

Saint Among the Hurons: The Life of John de Brébeuf (New
York, 1949), both happy combinations of careful investigation and a graceful literary style. Father Talbot's work
reveals intimate acquaintance with the source material but
the notes are awkwardly arranged in the back of the volumes.
Although old, the two volumes *Pioneer Priests of North
America 1642-1710* by Thomas J. Campbell, S.J. (New York,
1910, 1913) give interesting accounts of early Jesuit missionaries in individual portraits. The accounts are limited
to those who worked in New France. *The Jesuit Martyrs of
North America* John J. Wynn, S.J. (New York, 1925) is very
jejune, sketchy, and unsatisfactory. *An Autobiography of
Martyrdom. Spiritual Writings of the Jesuits in New France,*
edited by François Roustang, S.J., and translated by Sister
M. Renelle, S.S.N.D. (St. Louis, 1964) gives a vivid personal picture through the original documents of the intense
interior lives of the Jesuit missionaries in Canada. *Jacques Marquette, S.J. 1637-1675* by Joseph P. Donnelly, S.J.
(Chicago, 1968) gives a clear, orderly, and scholarly account of the famous missionary and explorer of the Mississippi. This volume includes photographs of several archival
documents that touch controverted points of Marquette's life,
one of which was the charge made about twenty-five years
ago that Marquette had not been ordained a priest. Fr.
Donnelly's assembly of evidence refutes that contention.
*The Jesuit Martyrs of Canada--Together with the Martyrs
Slain in the Mohawk Valley* by E. J. Devine, S.J. (Toronto,
1925), written by a competent historian on the occasion
of the beatification of the 8 French Jesuit martyrs of
Canada and New York, presents a chapter on each of the
beati as well as an introductory and a concluding chapter.

3. Europe

To the Other Towns by William V. Bangert, S.J.

(Westminster, Md., 1959) and *The Quiet Companion* by Mary
Purcell (Dublin, 1970) are scholarly and readable accounts
of the life of Blessed Pierre Favre, who in the judgment
of St. Ignatius was the supreme master of the Spiritual
Exercises among the first Jesuits. *James Lainez* by Joseph
H. Fichter, S.J. (St. Louis, 1944) is a reliable and clear
account of the Jesuit who succeeded St. Ignatius as general of the Society. *The Greatest of the Borgias* by Margaret Yeo (Milwaukee, 1936) is a clear recitation of the
life of St. Francis Borgia but is flawed by unhistorical
imaginings and pietistic style. *St. Peter Canisius* by
James Brodrick, S.J. (London, 1936, and Baltimore, 1950)
is a superbly written account of the second St. Boniface
of Germany, close to the sources, rich in background material, and sensitive to the problems of the early Society
of Jesus. *The Life and Work of Blessed Robert Francis
Cardinal Bellarmine, S.J., 1542-1621* by James Brodrick,
S.J. (2 volumes, London, 1928) is a magisterial portrait,
abundantly documented and delightfully written, of a leading figure of the Catholic Reform of the 16th and 17th centuries. *Robert Bellarmine. Saint and Scholar* (Westminster,
Md., 1961) is Father Brodrick's up-dated and abridged
edition of his earlier 2-volume masterpiece. *Bernadine
Realino. Renaissance Man* by Francis W. Sweeney, S.J. (New
York, 1951) is a sensitive portrayal of an attractive
pastoral saint but is overburdened in parts with historical background. *St. Alphonsus Rodriguez: Autobiography,*
translated by William Yeomans, S.J. (London, 1964), is an
important part of the fourteen books of spiritual writings
left by the coadjutor brother who spent most of his Jesuit
life as porter at the Jesuit college in Palma, Majorca.
No mystic of the Society of Jesus was so prolific a writer
as St. Alphonsus. Father Yeomans gives a sketch of Alphonsus' life and an appreciation of the value of the *Autobiograph*

as well as the translation. *St. Regis. A Social Crusader* *
by Albert S. Foley, S.J. (Milwaukee, 1941) is a well-told
account of the attractive French saint who died in 1640,
John Francis Regis. *St. John Berchmans* by the distinguished
Bollandist Hippolyte Delehaye, S.J., translated by Henry
Semple, S.J., (New York, 1921) and *A Modern Galahad. St.
John Berchmans* by Albert S. Foley, S.J. (Milwaukee, 1937)
are clear, straightforward, unpietistic accounts of the
Belgian scholastic who died in Rome in 1621, John Berchmans. The latter volume is based on earlier Flemish and
French works. A Flemish Jesuit who has specialized on the
life of St. John is Fr. K. Schoeters. In *Saint John Berchmans as Seen by his Contemporaries* James H. Gense, S.J.
(Bombay, 1949) presents much of the historical data gath-
ered by Fr. Schoeters. After some 25 years of reflection
on this subject, Fr. Schoeters presents a new work that
aims to explain to the modern reader St. John's preoccu-
pation with externals. It is *St. John Berchmans, the Shoe-
maker's Son*, adapted from the Flemish by James H. Gense,
S.J. (Bombay, 1965). *The Vocation of Aloysius Gonzaga* by
C. C. Martindale, S.J. (London, 1927) realistically portrays the young Italian saint in his reaction to the harsh
and corrupt milieu of the Renaissance. *Portrait of a
Champion* by Joseph E. Kerns, S.J. (Westminster, Md., 1957)
suffers in conviction because of the author's imaginative
expansion of the basic facts as he tries to fill out the
life of the Polish youth who died as a novice, St. Stanislaus Kostka. *Saint Stanislaus Kostka: A Psychological
Hagiography* by Joseph Majkowski, S.J. (Rome, 1972) is a
specialist's highly technical analysis of the saint. Despite its form as an unadapted thesis, it is readable. It
is a gold mine of factual data on formation in the early
Society of Jesus. *The life of Saint Andrew Bobola* by
Louis J. Gallagher, S.J., and P. V. Donovan, S.J., is
sketchy. *Perfect Friend: The Life of Blessed Claude La*

VI. *Biographies*

Colombière by Georges Guitton, S.J., translated by William
J. Young, S.J. (St. Louis, 1956) is a sensitive portrayal
of the spiritual director of St. Margaret Mary in her mission to spread devotion to the Sacred Heart of Jesus. *Faith-
ful Servant. Spiritual Retreats and Letters of Blessed
Claude La Colombière*, edited and translated by William J.
Young, S.J. (St. Louis, 1960), opens up the riches of the
interior life of the apostle of the Sacred Heart. *Good
Father in Brittany* by Martin Harney, S.J. (Boston, 1964)
tells in an interesting way the story of Blessed Julian
Maunoir with vivid descriptions of his missionary methods
in Brittany. *Man of Spain: Francis Suarez* by Joseph H.
Fichter, S.J. (New York, 1940) is an excellent popular
presentation of the life and works of one of the key figures
of the Spanish Renaissance of the 16th and 17th centuries.
*Life of Father Balthasar Alvarez, Religious of the Society
of Jesus* by Luis de Puente, S.J., unknown translator, 2
volumes, (London, 1868) is the classic life of the distinguished Spanish spiritual director of the 16th century
by another eminent master of the spiritual life. It includes Alvarez' teaching on prayer. *The Lives of Father
Paul Segneri, S.J., Father Peter Pinamonti, S.J., and the
Venerable John de Britto, S.J.* by Frederick Faber, (London,
1851) portrays the lives of three important Jesuits as
seen by a famous Oratorian of the 19th century. This collection, loaded down with ponderous sentences and with
pious phrases, presents two of the most influential Italian
preachers of the late 17th century and the Portuguese saint
who was martyred in India. *Herald of Christ: Louis Bour-
daloue* by John C. Reville, S.J. (New York, 1922) is a superficial and disappointing appreciation of one of the
greatest orators of The Great Century in France. *Blessed
Joseph Pignatelli, S.J.* by Florencio Zurbito, S.J., translated by J. C. Dias (Anand, India, 1933) is a short, clear,
straightforward account of the saint who cared so tenderly

48

for the Spanish Jesuits during the period of the suppression of the Society and started the restoration in Italy. *Blessed Joseph Pignatelli* by Daniel A. Hanly (New York, 1937 1937) is superficial, overdramatized, and romantic. *Edmund Campion* * by Evelyn Waugh (London, 1937) is a gracefully written portrayal of the charming priest who died at Tyburn in 1581. *The Life of Robert Southwell, Poet and Martyr* by Christopher Devlin, S.J. (New York, 1956) is a sensitive and perceptive relation of the life of a gentle and attractive poet and Elizabethan martyr. *An Appreciation of Robert Southwell* by Sister Rose Anita Morton (Philadelphia, 1929) is a scholarly and sensitive evaluation of Saint Robert, especially in his self-revelation in his poetry. *Henry Morse* by Philip Caraman, S.J. (London, 1957) is a quick moving account of the Jesuit martyr whose special apostolate was in the service of those stricken by epidemics. *Henry Garnet, 1555-1606, And the Gunpowder Plot* by Philip Caraman, S.J. (New York, 1964) is a lengthy, smooth, readable account of the superior of the English Jesuits, with special focus on the plot of some Catholics to blow up the Houses of Parliament. *The Autobiography of a Hunted Priest* by John Gerard, S.J., translated and edited by Philip Caraman, S.J. (New York, 1952) is the lively story of an enterprising priest in Elizabethan England who included among his exploits an escape from the Tower of London. *An Autobiography from the Jesuit Underground* by William Weston, S.J., translated and edited by Philip Caraman, S.J. (New York, 1955) is the personal story of a devout priest and Elizabethan prisoner whose holiness was widely recognized. *Martyr in Scotland* by Thomas Collins (London, 1955) is a clearly and interestingly told story of the life of Blessed John Ogilvie. *Francis Line, S.J. An Exiled English Scientist 1595-1675* by Connor Reilly, S.J. (Rome, 1969) is a scholarly presentation of Line's scientific work and his relations with the most eminent scientists of his day.

VI. Biographies

Letters and Memorials of Father Robert Persons, S.J.,
edited by Leo Hicks, S.J. (London, 1942), a meticulously
researched work, gives an excellent insight into the various attitudes and plans of Catholics vis-a-vis Elizabethan England. This volume covers Persons' writings only
to 1588. Two or more volumes are expected to cover the
remainder of this controversial Jesuit's life to 1610.
Distinguished Irishmen of the Sixteenth Century by Edmund
Hogan, S.J. (London, 1894) is a collection of sketches of
eighteen Irish Jesuits of the 1500's. Based on correspondence and other original documents, this clearly written
work gives a vivid picture of the Church's problems in the
Ireland of that age. *Roger Joseph Boscovich: Studies of
His Life and Work on the 250th Anniversary of His Birth*,
edited by Lancelot Whyte (London, 1961), a collection of
essays, includes a concise resume of the life of the most
distinguished of Jesuit scientists by Elizabeth Hill.
Jesuit Thinkers of the Renaissance, edited by Gerard Smith,
S.J. (Milwaukee, 1939), presents intellectual portraits of
six Jesuits with particular stress on a contribution made
by each to learning: Spanish Francisco Suárez, French
Dominic Bouhours, Spanish Luis de Molina, Belgian Leonard
Lessius, Spanish Juan de Mariana, Italian Robert Bellarmine.
Black and Red S.J. by Jerome Aixala, S.J. (Bombay, 1968)
is an interesting series of sketches of the 17 Jesuits who
were made cardinals up to 1959 (therefore excluding the
two raised by Pope Paul VI); the 5 who entered the Society
as cardinals; and the 4 who, after leaving the Society,
became cardinals. It also has the list of the 53 Jesuit
bishops living in 1962. *The Visions of Bernard Francis
De Hoyos, S.J.* by Henri Béchard, S.J. (New York, 1959) is
an uncritical and sugary account of a young Jesuit--he was
only 24 when he died--who was among the chief proponents
of devotion to the Sacred Heart of Jesus in early 18th-
century Spain. *Friedrich Spee's Trutznachtigall* by G.

D. *Post-suppression*

Richard Dimler, S.J. (Bern, 1973) is a scholarly and thorough study of the masterpiece of one of Germany's greatest
poets of the 17th century. Father Dimler presents a sensitive and penetrating synthesis of the many historical influences felt by Jesuit educators and spiritual writers
of the baroque era.

D. *Post-suppression*

The General Who Rebuilt the Jesuits by Robert North,
S.J. (Milwaukee, 1944) treats in a sugary and romanticized
way, without scholarly pretense, the life of Fr. John
Roothaan, the 21st General of the Society. *Father Rupert
Mayer* by Anton Koerbling, S.J., unknown translator (Cork,
1960), is a readable and informative account of the Jesuit
who as preacher, organizer of a mens' sodality, outspoken
foe of the Nazis, was a dynamic leader of Catholic life
in Munich before World War II. *Charles Dominic Plater,
S.J.* by C. C. Martindale, S.J. (London, 1922) is a well-
written portrayal of an English Jesuit who was intensely
involved in the social apostolate in the early 1900s. *Father Thurston* by Joseph H. Crehan, S.J. (London, 1952) is
a clear and orderly account of the Jesuit who became known
as a historian of Christian practices and as a scholar of
keen critical judgment. *Edmund Lester, S.J.* by Clement
Tiger, S.J. (London, 1937) is a popular and readable account of the founder of a famous school for delayed voca-
tions to the priesthood. *Bernard Vaughan, S.J.* by C.C. Martindale, S.J. (London, 1923) is an enjoyable biography of a
famous English preacher and lecturer who enjoyed controversy
and seemed "when not a child, a noisy boy, romping in God's
presence." *C. C. Martindale* by Philip Caraman, S.J. (London, 1967) gives a vivid and balanced picture of a bril-
liant classical scholar, cultivated popularizer of Catholic

subjects, and ardent champion of social justice. *Letters of Father de Clorivière 1787-1814*, edited by the Society of the Daughters of the Heart of Mary, unknown translator (New York, 1953), is a valuable collection, filling over 650 pages, of the letters written through 27 years, especially to Mlle. de Cicé, by a spiritual director *par excellence* and restorer of the Society of Jesus to post-Revolutionary France. *A Man after God's Own Heart. Life of Father Paul Ginhac, S.J.* by Arthur Calvet, S.J., translated by William Doyle, S.J. (London, 1914) is a smooth-running, a bit overly pious, account of the refined and timid Frenchman who for 40 years from mid-nineteenth century was novice master and tertian instructor, and who was widely revered for his sanctity and much sought for his direction. This life is a good example of a form of austere spirituality followed in the 19th century. *Alexis Clerc Sailor and Martyr* by Charles Daniel, S.J., translated by M.E.C.D., (New York, 1879) has a special value because of its account of the final days of Father Clerc, who was shot on 24 May 1871, one of the five Jesuits killed during the Paris Commune after the Franco-Prussian War. *The Happy Ascetic, Adoplph Petit* by Joseph R. N. Maxwell, S.J. (New York, 1936) is a short, popular life of a famous Belgian retreat master and tertian instructor of the early 20th century. *The Life of Father de Ravignan* by Armand de Ponlevoy, S.J., unknown translator (New York, 1869), although ponderous in style and apologetic in tone, nevertheless gives a good insight into the problems of the French Jesuits of the 19th century. Filled with quotations from the correspondence and the sermons of this effective preacher of Notre Dame in Paris, this volume gives through the stuffy prose of Father de Ravignan the temper of the moral and political climate and the response of this eminent spiritual leader. *A Memoir of Father Dignam* by Mother Mary Magdalen Taylor, S.M.G. (London, 1906) has a special value in the letters and observations of those who esteemed Father Dignam as a skilled spiritual director, since they give an inside view of a style of spiritual counselling of the late 19th century. *The Abate Juan Andres, Literary Historian of the XVIII Century* by Guido Ettore Mazzeo (New York, 1965), a scholarly, well-ordered, clearly written portrait of one of the leading Jesuits exiled from Spain in 1767, gives a good picture of how those Spanish exiles formed rich cultural communities in Italy. *God's Jester. The Story of Father Michael Pro, S.J.* by Mrs. George Norman (New York, 1930), a popular, quick-moving volume without scholarly apparatus to indicate the sources of the frequent quotations, vividly tells the history of the joyful and friendly priest who cared for the Catholic people during the Mexican persecutions of the 1920's and who died before the firing squad in November 1927. *Teilhard de Chardin. A Biographical Study* by Claude Cuénot, translated by Vincent Colimore (London, 1965), and *The Life of Teilhard de Chardin* by Robert Speaight (New York, 1967) are two of the better biographies among the abundant literature on the famous scientist-theologian. The work by Cuénot has the more ample scholarly apparatus as well as a 75 page bibliography of Teilhard's works, listed according to the year of their publication. *Father William Doyle, S.J. A Spiritual Study* by Alfred O'Rahilly (New York, 1925, 3rd edition, revised and enlarged), based on the journals of an Irish Jesuit who died in action during World War I, presents a vivid portrait of a spirituality that has the hallmark of Pelagianism. *John Baptist Franzelin, S.J.* by Nicholas Walsh, S.J. (Dublin, 1895) is a pious and uncritical sketch of the famous Swiss Jesuit theologian and cardinal who died in 1886. *Father Michael Browne, S.J., 1853-1933* by Thomas Hurley, S.J. (Dublin, 1949) tells in anecdotal and popular form the story of a widely known spiritual director in Ireland. *Life and Work of Rev. James*

VI. *Biographies*

Aloysius Cullen, S.J. by Lambert McKenna, S.J. (New York, 1924) is a popular and pious life of a priest best known in Ireland in the late 19th and early 20th centuries for his many pastoral works, especially in the Temperance movement. Many quotations from his spiritual diary and notes give the flavor of the ascetical emphasis of his spiritual direction. *Augustin Cardinal Bea: Spiritual Profile* edited by Stjepan Schmidt, S.J., translated by E. M. Steward (London, 1971), presents selections from Bea's diary, throwing light on the inner life of this busy churchman. These selections are limited to Bea's years as a cardinal. *Brother Francis Garate of the Society of Jesus 1857-1929* by Juan Perez Arregui, S.J., translated by Francis Corley, S.J. (New York, 1942), tells in a simple and direct way the uneventful life of the brother who as door keeper at the Jesuit University of Deusto in Bilbao resembled the canonized doorkeeper of the Jesuit college in Palma, St. Alfonso Rodriguez. *Gerard Manley Hopkins: Priest and Poet* by John Pick (New York, 1942; 2nd edition * 1966) is both a concise record of Hopkins' life and a detailed exposition of his poetry. *Gerard Manley Hopkins: A Study of His Ignatian Spirit* by David A. Downes (New York, 1959) is a scholarly study of St. Ignatius' influence on Hopkins. *Father Constant Lievens, S.J.* by Francis J. Bowen (St. Louis, 1936) narrates in a brief and popular style the life of the young Belgian Jesuit--only 38 when he died in 1895--who was singularly successful in his missionary labors in Chota-Nagpur in India. There are at least two lives of Father John Sullivan, S.J., who was the son of Sir Edward Sullivan, Lord Chancellor of Ireland during the latter 19th century, and a convert to the Catholic Church at the age of 35. The first, *The Port of Tears. The Life of Father John Sullivan, S.J.* by Mathias Bodkin, S.J. (Dublin, 1954) is short, crisp, and sprinkled with pious phraseology. The second,

Father John Sullivan, S.J, by Fergal McGrath, S.J., is
longer, more detailed, including judgments by his contemporaries. *Father Francis Tarin, S.J.* by J. Dissard, S.J.,
translated by Katherine Henvey (London, 1928) is a short,
anecdotal, pious record of a preacher and confessor in the
rural areas of Spain. *The Prison Meditations of Father Alfred Delp,* translator not given (New York, 1963) is, in the
words of Thomas Merton, who contributes an Introduction,
"a penetrating diagnosis of a devastated, gutted, faithless
society in which man is rapidly losing his humanity" by the
Jesuit who was executed in the Plotzensee prison on Febru-
ary 2, 1945, by the Nazis. *Guerrilla Padre in Mindanao* by
Edward Haggerty, S.J. (New York, 1946) tells in a very detailed way Father Haggerty's activities with some of the
Filipinos who successfully evaded the Japanese troops during
their occupation of the Philippines during World War II.
Memorial of the Life and Death of Fr. Augustus Law by an
anonymous author (London, 1883) leads the way in a very
short list of old biographies of Jesuits in Africa, and
gives the record of the dogged determination in the face
of debilitating heat and crippling sickness of the English
Jesuit who died at Umzila's Kraal in 1880. Most of this
record is found in the more up-to-date *Gubulawayo and Beyond,* edited by Michael Gelfand (London, 1968), which is
more amply noted in the section of this bibliography on
Africa. *Life of Augustus Law* by Ellis Schreiber (London,
1893) fills out the account in the previous title. *Thirty
Years in the African Wilds* by E. Vervimp, S.J., translated by
W. Peters, S.J. and M. Hannan, S.J., (London, 1938) is the
life of Brother de Sadleer, S.J., one of the outstanding
of the pioneer missionaries in Rhodesia and the Congo.
Henry Schomberg Kerr. Sailor and Jesuit by Mrs. Maxwell
Scott (London, 1901) tells the story of the second superior
in the 19th century Zambezi mission. *The Yellow River Runs
Red. Bl. René Isoré, Modestus Andlauer, Leo Mangin and Paul*

Denn (Jesuit Martyrs) by F. X. Froehly, S.J. (Tiruchira-palli, India, 1955) tells in a brief and popular way the story of the Jesuits who were murdered during the Boxer Rebellion in China.

E. *The United States*

I Lift My Lamp, edited by John P. Leary, S.J. (West-minster, Md., 1955), is a wide-ranging and popular col-lection of the lives of 16 Jesuits who labored within the area of the present United States. Among the 16 are Arnold Damen, Carl Hausmann, Richard Tierney, Eusebio Kino. *Wilder-ness Kingdom. The Journals and Paintings of Father Nicolas Point*, translated by Joseph P. Donnelly, S.J. (New York, 1967) gives the personal recollections and the paintings of a French Jesuit who worked among the Indians of the Rocky Mountains in mid-19th century. Father Point's paint-ings, exquisitely reproduced in this large and beautiful volume, have a vividness and simplicity in their lines and color that make them an authentic record of Indian life. *General Sherman's Son* by Joseph T. Durkin, S.J. (New York, 1959) is the story, well-told by a careful historian, of the erratic Jesuit son of one of the more famous generals of the Northern armies during the Civil War. Father Sherman died in 1933. *A Moulder of Men. John H. O'Rourke, S.J.* by W. Coleman Nevils, S.J. (New York, 1953) abounds in rhetori-cal flourish as it unfolds the life of a famous novice mas-ter, retreat director, editor of the *Sacred Heart Messenger*, who died in 1929. This volume has many examples of Father O'Rourke's articles and sermons, which were characterized by a highly dramatic kind of presentation. *Richard H. Tierney, S.J.* by Francis X. Talbot, S.J. (New York, 1930) is a short and direct account of the life of a Jesuit who became known as an aggressive and combative editor of

America in the 1920's. *The Manner Is Ordinary* by John LaFarge, S.J. (New York, 1954) is Father LaFarge's auto-biography. A work of literary finesse, it recounts the experiences of a highly intelligent and cultivated priest who worked among the Blacks of Maryland, edited *America*, and was absorbed in interests as diverse as liturgical re-form, interracial justice, world peace. Father LaFarge wrote a continuation and amplification of this work in his pleasant and thoughtful autobiographical *An American Amen: A Statement of Hope* (New York, 1958). *Reverend Carlos M. Pinto, S.J. Apostle of El Paso 1892-1919* by Sister M. Lil-liana Owens (El Paso, 1951) is a simple and direct story of a priest who made a deep impression among the people of El Paso, Texas, for 27 years. This volume, filled with apt quotations of primary sources and with pictures, also tells in good measure the story of the Catholic Church in El Paso. *Most Reverend Anthony J. Schuler, S.J.* by Sister Lilliana Owens (El Paso, 1953) is a clear, simple, and amply docu-mented story of the pioneering work of the first bishop of El Paso, who for 27 years built up his diocese. As she did in her volume on Father Pinto, Sister Lilliana gives an abundance of interesting photographs. Bishop Schuler re-tired in 1942. *A Memoir of Father Felix Joseph Barbelin, S.J.* by Eleanor C. Donnelly (Philadelphia, 1886) is a pious, anecdotal, and heavily rhetorical volume on the founder of St. Joseph's College in Philadelphia, who deserves a much better memorial of his achievements. *Journal of Father Adam Marshall 1824-1825*, edited by Joseph T. Durkin, S.J. (Scranton, 1943), contains the observations of the first chaplain of the U.S. Navy during his tour of duty in the *USS North Carolina*. Father Marshall died aboard his ship and was buried in the Mediterranean on 20 September 1825. *Arnold Damen, S.J.* by J. Conroy, S.J. (New York, 1930) is a popular account, including several letters, of the Dutch Jesuit who was active in the Mid-west during the middle of

the 19th century as a missionary preacher, and who was
closely tied to the thriving Holy Family parish of Chicago
and the foundation of St. Ignatius College there. The author calls the volume "a chapter in the making of Chicago."
Father Finn, S.J. The Story of His Life Told by Himself,
edited by Daniel A. Lord, S.J. (New York, 1929), is the
simply told autobiography of Father Francis Finn, best
known for his 27 books for young people and their evoca-
tion of memories of Jesuit schools in the late 19th century. Some of his titles are *Tom Playfair, Claude Light-
foot, Cupid of Campion*, and *The Best Foot Forward. Life,
Letters, and Travels of Father Pierre-Jean De Smet, S.J.
1801-1873*, edited by Hiram M. Chittenden and Alfred T.
Richardson, 4 volumes (New York, 1905), is a neatly balanced biographical account and edition of the correspondence of the outstanding Jesuit among the American Indians
of the 19th century. These volumes are a good source to
learn about De Smet's quick and sharp perception of details
of people, geography, animals, rivers, and the like. *The
Life of Father De Smet* by E. Laveille, S.J., translated by
Marian Lindsay (New York, 1915) is a reliable, quick-moving
narrative, filled with many quotations from De Smet's vivid
reports. *Father De Smet* by Helene Margaret (New York, 1940)
is marred by its fictional parts and the imagined conversa-
tions. *Edmund A. Walsh, S.J.* by Louis J. Gallagher, S.J.
(New York, 1962) tells the story in a popular way and without the help of critical apparatus of one of the more influential American Jesuits of the first half of the 20th century, who founded the School of Foreign Service of Georgetown
University, headed the Papal Relief Mission in Russia during
the famine of 1922-1924, and acted as consultant to Justice
Jackson at the Nuremberg trials. *William Pardow of the Com-
pany of Jesus* by Justine Ward (New York, 1915) recalls in a
popular and rather eulogistic way one of the most vigorous
Jesuit preachers of the East during the late 19th and early
20th centuries. *Life and Letters of Henry Van Rensselaer*

by Edward P. Spillane, S.J. (New York, 1908) is a simple
and uncritical story of a Jesuit who was prominent in the
pastoral life of New York City, especially among the fire-
men, during the late 19th and early 20th centuries. *Elo-
quent Indian. The Life of James Bouchard, California Jesuit*
by John B. McGloin, S.J. (Stanford, 1949) is a full-length
and scholarly study of an American Indian who became a
Jesuit and an outstanding figure in the Far West in the
late 19th century. Of him at his death Patrick Riordan,
the second Archbishop of San Francisco, said: "To no man
of all the West is the Church of God more beholden than to
Father James Bouchard of the Society of Jesus." *Dominic
Giacobbi, A Noble Corsican* by Richard A. Gleeson, S.J.
(New York, 1938) presents in a popular and pious way the
life of an influential and widely loved Jesuit of the
California Province who died in 1930. *Played by Ear* by
Daniel A. Lord, S.J. (Chicago, 1956) is Father Lord's autobiography, written in his fast-moving and jaunty style, in
which he gives a vivid picture of his work with the Sodality
of the Blessed Virgin Mary. *Father Pierre Bouscaren, S.J.
A Spiritual Autobiography*, edited by William L. Hornsby,
S.J. (Milwaukee, 1935), consists of extracts from the spiritual journals and correspondence of a Jesuit teacher who,
despite serious sickness, was singularly determined to
achieve a high holiness. He died in 1927. The editor
provides a brief sketch of Father Bouscaren's life. *The
Life and Letters of Walter Drum, S.J.* by Joseph Gorayeb,
S.J. (New York, 1928), while without scholarly apparatus,
is filled with many selections from the writings and correspondence of a vigorous and vital lecturer on Scripture,
who died in 1921. *Father Shealy--A Tribute* by Gerald C.
Treacy, S.J. (New York, 1927) is a short and popularly
written account of the Jesuit who in New York in 1909
started the Laymen's Retreat Movement in the United States.
One of the most important figures in the Church of the early

United States was John Carroll, first Archbishop of Baltimore, who had been a Jesuit before the Suppression of the
Society and who encouraged the Society's restoration in
the United States. Two scholarly lives of this key figure
in American Jesuit history are *The Life and Times of John
Carroll* by Peter Guilday (New York, 1922) and *John Carroll
of Baltimore 1735-1815* by Annabelle M. Melville (New York,
1955). *Better A Day*, edited by John Leary, S.J. (New York,
1951) is a series of vignettes in popular style of Jesuit
brothers in the United States. *With God in Russia* by
Walter Ciszek, S.J. (New York, 1964) gives Father Ciszek's
personal story, vividly told, of his early life in the Society, his incursion into Russia after the latter's inva-
sion of Poland in 1939, his capture and imprisonment, including 15 years in a Siberian prison camp. Fr. Ciszek
follows up this work with his spiritual reflections on his
Russian ordeal in *He Leadeth Me* (New York, 1973). *I Was
Chaplain on the "Franklin"* by Joseph O'Callahan, S.J., is
a fast-moving account of Father O'Callahan's stint as a
naval chaplain in World War II, with emphasis on the ordeal
of the *USS Franklin* off the coast of Japan. *Jesuits as
Chaplains in the Armed Forces 1917-1960* ** by Gerard F.
Giblin, S.J. (Woodstock, Md., 1961) is basically a collection of short biographical notices of the Jesuits who
served in the American military forces from World War I to
the post-Korean War period. It includes a list of cita-
tions and awards. *Rev. Joseph M. Cataldo, S.J.* by George
F. Weibel, S.J. (Spokane, 1928) is a short sketch of a
colorful Italian missionary in the Northwest. *A Yankee
Xavier. Henry P. McGlinchey, S.J.* by Neil Boyton, S.J.
(New York, 1937) records in a simple and uncritical way
the life of an American Jesuit who died in India in 1918.
A Memoir. Richard A. Gleeson, S.J. 1861-1945 by Alexander
Cody, S.J. (San Francisco, 1950) is an unrelieved recita-
tion of praise, and so hampers a genuine picture of a

distinguished pastor and educator of the California Province. *Memoir of the Life of Rev. Burchard Villiger of the Society of Jesus* by John J. Ryan, S.J. (Philadelphia, 1906) relates in a plain way, almost in chronicle fashion, the story of one of the more influential pastors of the Gesu in Philadelphia during the late 19th century. *A Memoir of William A. Stanton, S.J.* by William T. Kane, S.J. (St. Louis, 1918) records the story of an impressive missionary to the Philippines and Belize, who died when only 40 years old, a story that is flawed by pious asides and unctuous phrases. A redeeming feature is the ample quoting from Father Stanton's correspondence. *The Story of the Romance* by William E. Rively, S.J. (New York, 1953) is a chatty, informal, quick moving narrative in which the author tells of his missionary labors in the Caroline Islands on his ship *Romance* after World War II. *In The Presence of My Enemies* by John W. Clifford, S.J. (New York, 1963) is Father Clifford's personal account, vividly told, of his experience as a prisoner of the Chinese Communists after World War II. *I Met a Traveller. The Triumph of Father Phillips* by Kurt Becker, S.J. (New York, 1958) is a quick moving and graphic account of the ordeal of a California Jesuit during his imprisonment by the Chinese Communists. *Father Dave. David Plante McAstocker, S.J.* by Wilfred P. Schoenberg, S.J. (Milwaukee, 1960) is a sentimental and uncritical account of a Jesuit of the Oregon Province who carried on an apostolate of popular religious writing despite serious sickness. *The Story of Dan Lyons, S.J.*, by John D. McCallum (New York, 1973) is an uncritical and adulatory account, with many pictures, of the priest who was strongly identified with ultraconservative thought in the Church during the 1960s and early 1970s and who in 1975 left the Society. *Father Ravalli's Missions* by Harold Allen (Chicago, 1972) is an artistic and architectural study of some of the mission stations of Fr. Anthony

Ravalli, one of the outstanding Italian Jesuits who worked in the American Northwest during the late 19th century. The author treats in an instructive way the style of the buildings, the windows, the statues, the altars. A number of photographs clarify the text.

PART VII. SOME APOSTOLATES

Jesuit Education. An Essay on the Foundations of Its Idea by John W. Donohue, S.J. (New York, 1963), "a modest and tentative [author's words] inquiry into the abiding spirit which fashioned the great documents standing at the beginning of the Society of Jesus's history," is a gracefully written study of the original Jesuit educational ideas and their implementation in history. *The Jesuit Code of Liberal Education* by Allan P. Farrell, S.J. (Milwaukee, 1938) is a large technical study of the steps that led to the formulation of the *Ratio Studiorum* of 1599. There is also a chapter on the revised *Ratio Studiorum* of 1832. *Saint Ignatius' Idea of a Jesuit University* by George E. Ganss, S.J. (Milwaukee, 1956) presents a balanced and perceptive study "toward discovering more clearly what were St. Ignatius' educational principles which may be classified as perennial." It has an English translation of Part IV of the Constitutions of the Society of Jesus, which treats the education of Jesuits and lay students. The application of those principles through the *Ratio Studiorum* and the history of the widespread Jesuit educational system, even into the United States, is succinctly sketched by the same author in *The Jesuit Educational Tradition and St. Louis University. Some Bearings for the University's Sesquicentennial 1818-1969.* (St. Louis, 1969). *The Jesuits and Education* by William J. McGucken, S.J. (Milwaukee, 1932) is an analysis, scholarly and clearly presented, of Jesuit teaching principles and practices, especially in secondary education in the United States of the 1930s and before. See also the histories of various Jesuit colleges and universities, above on page 32.

Abridged History of the Sodalities of Our Lady by Émile Villaret, S.J., translated by William J. Young, S.J. (St. Louis, 1956) is a concentrated version of Father Villaret's much larger history of the Sodalities of the Blessed Virgin Mary.

The Apostleship of Prayer by Henri Ramière, translator unknown (New York, 1898) is a short account of the apostolate founded on devotion to the Sacred Heart in the 19th century France and advanced so successfully by Father Ramière.

The Work of the Bollandists Through Three Centuries 1615-1915 by Hippolyte Delehaye, S.J., unknown translator (Princeton, 1922) is a short and authoritative account of the great historical enterprise of the Belgian Jesuits on the lives of the saints. Father Delehaye is one of the most eminent of these Belgian scholars. David Knowles, former Regius Professor of Modern History at Cambridge University, expresses his sensitive appreciation of the Bollandists in the first chapter of his *Great Historical Enterprises* (London, 1963), where he writes of them as "the first great enterprise of co-operative scholarship in the modern world; and theirs is the only enterprise of the seventeenth century which still continues in active function."

Jesuit Mission Presses in the Pacific Northwest. A History and Bibliography of Imprints 1876-1899 by Wilfred P. Schoenberg, S.J. (Portland, 1957) is a scholarly tool for understanding the problems the Jesuits faced in operating printing presses on the American frontier. *Optimus Magister Bonus Liber*, author unknown (Chicago, 1953) is a short and beautiful tribute to the craftmanship of Loyola University Press in its 40th year and to its able editor, Father Austin G. Schmidt, S.J., on his 50th year as a Jesuit.

Jesuits and Music. A Study of Musicians Connected with the German College in Rome during the 17th Century and their Activities in Northern Europe by Thomas D. Culley, S.J. (Rome, 1970) is a scholarly and illuminating volume about the influence of one of the key Jesuit institutions in Rome. *The Fine Arts in the Old Society: A Preliminary Investigation* by Clement J. McNaspy, S.J. and Thomas D. Culley, S.J. (Rome, 1972) is a meticulous and thorough study that concentrates chiefly on music among the Jesuits during the generalates of St. Ignatius and Diego Laynez. It is an expansion of an article that appeared originally in *Archivum Historicum Societatis Jesu*, Vol. 40 (1971), pp. 213-245. Father McNaspy recalls some of the more important facts in this article in "Art in Jesuit Life" in *Studies in the Spirituality of Jesuits* (Vol. V, no. 3, April, 1973). *Baroque Art: The Jesuit Contribution*, edited by Rudolf Wittkower and Irma Jaffe (New York, 1972), contains several illuminating articles by authorities in the fields of painting, architecture, and music, as well as 64 plates. *Oxford Companion to Art*, edited by Harold Osborne (11th edition, Oxford, 1970), has a clear and succinct article under the title "Baroque." *Oxford Companion to the Theatre*, edited by Phyllis Hartnoll (3rd edition, Oxford, 1967), has a well-ordered and informative article on Jesuit drama done by Edna Purdie under the title "Jesuit Drama." *Patrons and Painters. A Study in the Relations between Italian Art and Society in the Age of the Baroque* by Francis Haskell (New York, 1963) gives considerable attention to the Jesuits and their problemns with their benefactors, especially in the building and decorating of the Churches of the Gesù and Sant' Ignazio in Rome. *Religious Art from the Twelfth to the Eighteenth Century* * by Émile Mâle, translator not given, (New York, 1958), with 48 plates, has a special value in that it presents the art of the Tridentine and post-Tridentine periods in its relations to the art of the medieval centuries.

PART IX.   DOCTORAL DISSERTATIONS

During the past few years, several doctoral dissertations have been written on various aspects of the Society,
educational, financial, pastoral, religious. Listed here
are only those that either completely or in large part
treat of the Society's history. These may be obtained in
positive microfilm and softbound xerographic copies at
Xerox University Microfilms, Ann Arbor, Michigan, 48106.
The symbol DAI refers to the place in *Dissertation Ab-
stracts International*, where a synopsis of a particular
thesis may be found. *The Expulsion of the Jesuits from
the Vice-royalty of New Granada 1767* by Charles J. Fleener,
University of Florida (Gainesville, 1969) DAI 31 (1970-
1971) 2303 A; *Father Gregory Mengarini, an Italian Jesuit
Missionary in the Transmontane West: His Life and Memoirs*
by Gloria R. Lothrop, University of Southern California
(Los Angeles, 1970) DAI (1970-1971) 2286 A; *The Jansenists
and the Expulsion of the Jesuits from France, 1757-1765*
by Dale K. Van Kley, Yale University (New Haven, 1970)
DAI 32 (1971-1972) 373 A; *The Distribution of the Expro-
priated Jesuit Properties in Mexico, with Special Reference
to Chihuahua, 1767-1777* by Harold B. Benedict, University
of Washington (Seattle, 1970) DAI 32 (1971-1972) 336 A;
The Anti-Christian Persecution of 1616-1617 in Nanking by
Edward T. Kelly, Columbia University (New York, 1971) DAI
32 (1971-1972) 1427 A; *The Confiscation and Administration
of Jesuit Property under the Jurisdiction of the Parlement
of Paris, 1762-1798* by Dorothy G. Thompson, University of
British Columbia, 1972) DAI 33 (1972-1973) 4322 A; *The
Evolution of the Jesuit Mission System in Northwestern
New Spain, 1600-1767* by Charles W. Polzer, S.J., University
of Arizona (Tucson, 1972) DAI 33 (1972-1973) 5102 A; *The
Management of the Estates of the Jesuit Colegio Maximo de
San Pedro y San Pablo of Mexico City in the Eighteenth*

Century by James D. Riley, Tulane University (New Orleans, 1972) DAI 33 (1972-1973) 1126 A; *The Impact of the Jesuits' Estates Act on Canadian Politics, 1888-1891* by James R. Miller, University of Toronto (Toronto, 1972) DAI 34 (1973-1974) 5069 A.

INDEX

The Numbers refer to pages

Index

Ives, J. Moss, 20

J

Jacobsen, Jerome V., 17
Jaffe, Irma, 65
Jogues, St. Isaac, 44
Johnson, Samuel, 13
Josephy, Alvin M., Jr., 30
Joset, Joseph, 30
Jury, Wilfrid, 18

K

Kane, William T., 61
K'ang-hsi, Emperor of China, 22
Kay, Hugh, 37
Kelly, Edward T., 66
Kennedy, John H., 18
Kenny, Michael, 16, 32
Kenton, Edna, 17
Kenyon, John, 27
Kerns, Joseph E., 47
Kerr, Henry Shomberg, 55
Kerr, Ralph F., 3
Kessell, John L., 16, 42
Kidd, Kenneth E., 18
Kino, Eusebio 15, 41, 42, 43, 56
Kley, Dale Van, 28, 66
Kneller, Karl, 10
Knowles, David, 4, 64
Koerbling, Anton, 51
Konscak, Ferdinand, 44
Korth, Eugene H., 13
Kostka, St. Stanislaus, 47
Krahl, Joseph, 22
Kratz, Wilhelm, 10

L

Lach, Donald F., 20
La Farge, John, 8, 20, 29, 57
Laimbeckhoven, Gottfried X. von, 22
Laínez, James, 46
Latourette, Kenneth S., 6
Laures, Johannes, 23
La Valette, Antoine, 28
Laveille, E., 58
Law, Augustus, 55
Leary, John P., 56, 60
Leite, Serafim, 14

Lessius, Leonard, 50
Lester, Edmund, 51
Leturia, Pedro de, 35, 38
Lewis, Clifford M., 17
Ley, Charles D., 12
Lievens, Constant, 54
Linck, Wenceslaus, 43
Lindsay, Marian, 58
Line, Francis, 49
Llorente, Segundo, 31
Lobo, Jeronimo, 13
Loomie, Albert J., 17
Lord, Daniel, 37, 58, 59
Lothrop, Gloria R., 66
Lucey, William L., 30
Lunn, Arnold, 41
Lyons, Daniel, 61

M

McAstocker, David, 61
McCallum, John D., 61
McGlinchey, Henry P., 60
McGloin, John B., 33, 59
McGrath, Fergal, 55
McGucken, William J., 63
McKenna, Lambert, 54
McKevitt, Gerald, 32
Maclagen, Edward, 24
McNaspy, Clement J., 65
Majkowski, Joseph, 47
Male, Emile, 65
Mangin, Bl. Leo, 55
Margaret, Helene, 58
Mariana, Juan de, 50
Marquette, Jacques, 19, 45
Marshall, Adam, 57
Martin, A. Lynn, 27
Martin, Luis, 15
Martindale, C.C., 13, 41, 47, 51
Matt, Leonard von, 35
Matthieu, Claude, 27
Maunoir, Bl. Julian, 48
Maxwell, Joseph R.N., 52
Mayer, Rupert, 51
Maynard, Theodore, 2
Mazzeo, Guido Ettore, 53
Meadows, Denis, 2
Meagher, Walter J., 32
Mealing, S.R., 17
Meenan, Daniel F.X., 1
Melville, Annabelle M., 60
Mengarini, Gregorio, 30, 66

125

GENERAL BOOKBINDING CO.

79   137NY2   4   340   A   6108

QUALITY CONTROL MARK